The Hope & Joy That Discovering God Gives Our Lives

Anthony Lambert

BALBOA.
PRESS

A DIVISION OF HAY HOUSE

Balboa Press books may be ordered through booksellers or by contacting:

Balboa Press
A Division of Hay House
1663 Liberty Drive
Bloomington, IN 47403
www.balboapress.com.au
1 (877) 407-4847

Print information available on the last page.

ISBN: 978-1-5043-1123-6 (sc)
ISBN: 978-1-5043-1124-3 (e)

Balboa Press rev. date: 01/26/2018

TABLE OF CONTENTS

PREFACE

Trust and hope in God's guidance and help in your life

Before reading this book, it is necessary to OPEN YOUR HEART AND MIND think and reflect on what you believe about God, is He real for you? Try to establish where you are at and what you actually believe. Try to approach what is presented in this book with an open mind. **I sincerely hope that you learn something that you can actually use in your life that opens your mind and heart and becomes very meaningful to you.**

What in fact do you think and feel ?-----Do you believe that there is ----------------

1. ---**A God or Gods - Supreme beings.** - What influence do they have on us and in our world?

2. ---**A life other than our earthly life?** --- What does this mean to you?

3. -- **A Devil or evil Gods.** -- What is our relationship with them? Can they hurt us?

4. ---**No God at all** --- that what we see and experience magically happened by chance----- the result of **NATURAL EVOLUTION**

Where did we come from and what caused our creation? What do you think and feel about religious books? The Bible---The Koran---The Torah---Buddha's writings---Hinduism---Etc. Millions of people all over the world live their lives according to these teachings and form their beliefs so strongly that they are prepared to fight and die for their beliefs, both in our present day and for thousands of years past. **WHY?** Are they just gullible? What is the truth in these writings and what do they mean for us? Do you have any opinion? It is of fundamental importance to take the time and make the effort to think it through for yourself.

WHAT INDEED ARE OUR LIVES ALL ABOUT ?

We are individually responsible for our lives. It is stupid to blame others for how we live our lives. WE HAVE A FREE WILL AND HOW WE USE THIS IS OUR CHOICE.

It is a complete "Cop Out" to say. My -----Friends, Parents, Teachers, social position, Upbringing, Education or lack thereof, Life experience, Etc. Etc.-------caused me to be what I am and believe what I believe.----- I can not think or act otherwise.

Each of us is the Captain of our own destiny and what we make of our lives really depends on us ---- IN THE CHOICES THAT WE MAKE

All of life is a balancing act. I believe it is a significant achievement to remain sane and well adjusted mentally from the cradle to the grave. It is very easy to fall into states of apathy, over reaction, anxiety, fear and deep depression. Balance and moderation are our keys to success, but are not easily maintained.

This book promotes BELIEF AND TRUST IN GOD AND IN HIS HELP IN OUR LIVES. GOD is our major resource He becomes the tool we can use to guide and help us throughout our lives if we but trust and open ourselves to Him.

YOU CAN ESTABLISH A TRUE ONE TO ONE RELATIONSHIP WITH GOD IF YOU TRY

What you make of this book will depend on you. I hope and trust that it helps you throughout your life to find your path to God, so that your soul (your immortal spirit) can share complete happiness for all eternity with the God who created all of us.

AUTHOR'S NOTE

Trust and hope in God's guidance and help in your life

All of us arrive in this world and personally experience it's realities as they happen to us. **THIS IS THE CONTENT OF OUR LIFE** What we think and conclude about this as we mature and reflect on our lives, sooner or later prompts questions that occur and reoccur in our lives.-

QUESTIONS LIKE

- How did I get here and what caused my existence?

- Is there any purpose in my life or for my life? When I realise that **I am one only of approx. seven thousand million people on this planet.**

- How did all that I experience in my reality come into being? What or who caused this creation?

- What purpose is there for all other people, all living creatures? Is the reality I perceive **REAL** and what effect does it have in my life and on my life?

- What control do I have over all that I perceive?

- Can I have **joy, happiness and HOPE** in my life?

- Is what I see and perceive **ALL THAT THERE IS?**

- Is there a supreme entity-------**GOD?**

These questions or similar gradually occur and reoccur to most of us sooner or later in our lives. The search for answers can occupy our whole lives. **Where are you at in your life? Have you reached any conclusions?**

This book shares with you the results of my search and thinking about the above which **finally** caused me to choose to be a practising Catholic. Originally, I inherited Catholicism from my parents, this meant very little to me in my early life, still I was grateful to my parents for providing me with a **starting position and frame of reference** to explore my spiritually and try to establish how things truly are for me.

After a lifetime of searching, I have confirmed in my mind that there is a God, that He initiated / caused the creation of all that we perceive in our reality and that the major purpose of our lives is to find our way back to Him by obeying His will for us, so that we can earn and enjoy the eternal happiness –– THAT HE PROMISES US.

The fact that I have now confirmed in my mind that there is a God and chosen to be a Catholic does not mean that this is the only way (or indeed that this is the best way) to find a path to God, or that Catholic teaching is the only truth. I have chosen this path, after trying other ways, as this path feels comfortable and right for me and -

I AM SURE THIS IS A TRUE AND CORRECT PATH TO GOD.

I am now however convinced that God accepts people who follow other paths, what counts is what is in their hearts and how they obeyed God's will for them. Our **free will** allows us to make choices about what we do. **NOTE HOWEVER THAT** our choices include all the elements contained in their make up, our personal resources (abilities, talents, intelligence, etc.) and material resources (wealth, power, social position, influence and so forth) **and**

OUR CHOICES ARE UNIQUE FOR EACH OF US.

WE however, have a responsibility directly to God and He will hold us accountable for the choices we have made in our lives. He will consider ALL the elements involved in our choices and will Judge us on the choices we have made. HE will then decide on our place in eternity.

I believe all Christian religions, Judaism, Islam and even some eastern religions such as Buddhism can in fact be legitimate paths to God, I believe that God in fact inspired (gave power to) the founders of these religions to inspire and lead large numbers of us back to Him.

People like Jesus Christ (Christianity), Mohammed (Islam), Buddha (Buddhism) and so forth would not have succeeded without God's help and blessing.

The books that form the basis, beliefs, history and teachings of these religions have been handed down to us by our ancestors (BIBLE, KORAN, TORAH, ETC.) Our ancestors lived their lives developing and refining what they believed and that what was written in these books was inspired by God.

It is very difficult now to know with complete certainty the exact detail and accuracy of what was written (when and by who) and how we should respond to conflicts and discrepancies in the text of any one particular book, let alone all of them

Also the credibility of these books when compared with what we have learned in our searches, research and investigations into our origin, our world and our universe requires review and thought to confirm that what is written is possible, makes sense and is not beyond reason when detail comparisons are made.

NOTE: Belief in GOD does not require a perfect match with all of what is written in these books and our comparison with scientific discoveries. Discrepancies that we perceive however should not destroy our faith in God.

We in fact need God infinitely more than He needs us. Our task is to find God, love Him and obey His will for us, ask yourself "WHAT DOES GOD WANT FROM ME?"

Our responsibility is always directly to God and we are individually responsible to Him for all that we do. When I think about God, I wonder about how He can have a personal relationship with each and every one of us, something like seven thousand million of us living on this planet (7 000 000 000).How can God know what happens in each of our lives, the fine balance between forces present, people involved, resources available and the problems which we face. Is there any point in praying to Him for comfort, guidance and support?

-DOES HE REALLY KNOW US, AND CAN-
-- HE ACTUALLY HELP US?

How is it possible for Him to help and respond to us effectively on a personal basis? The practicalities of this at our current state of knowledge appear to make this impossible, yet throughout our history many of us appear to have known God on a personal level and the various holy books (Bible, Koran, Torah, Etc.) all tell us that God can and does respond to us as individuals. To believe God knows us, does hear our prayers and responds directly to us for me requires at least the possibility of some sort of credible explanation (I don't believe in fairy tales). The marvels of computer technology can perhaps give us inklings as to how this could be possible, for example computers handle the individual accounts of millions of us, countless 4 transactions, yet each of us receives our own statement showing all transactions we initiated or that effected our accounts, a **personal statement for each of us even though we are one only of millions of account holders.** One hundred years ago what we can now achieve with our technology would have been considered impossible, a complete and hopeless pipe dream yet here we are doing what was then considered impossible.

Our knowledge and understanding is increasing in volume and accuracy and shows us possibilities of HOW GOD could respond to us as individuals. I believe that GOD is revealing more and more of the truth of Himself and His creation to us, we are getting glimpses of the big picture. In reflecting on how we should serve our God. I believe it is not necessary to as it were **"reinvent the wheel."** Countless millions of people have lived and died before us, many of whom thought about and struggled to understand what their lives were all about, what their relationship with God was and indeed what it should be? Their struggles and deliberations produced the major religions with I believe God's prompting and blessing.

Following an organised religion, **<u>but with love and obedience to God as our complete and primary motivation makes sense,</u>** as this enables us to use what other sincere followers of God thought about and lived through. With our thinking brains we can use, refine and build on their experience and efforts. **Our responsibility however, is always directly to God for all that we choose in our lives.** His commands to us to love Him and our fellow men must never be contradicted by anything we read in books, **or by following leaders who may be charismatic, powerful, persuasive and credible, but do not follow God's basic commands. We however must choose and accept responsibility for what we do or don't do.**

Love of GOD and our fellow men is an ABSOLUTE and all other teaching, books and rationale must support this, as this is God's fundamental requirement of us.

Religions are beliefs, techniques and practices established by our ancestors in their search for God and passed on to us. **Some appear to be the direct result of God making actual contact with the founders of these religions and if this is true then they are extremely beneficial to us because they are God's will revealed.** Furthermore, they have evolved in most cases from the actions of sincere and good people following God's will as they understood it to the best of their ability. **We can certainly learn and profit from their experience, use and build on this, to find our path to God.**

The exact detail of God, is not as important as -- LOVING HIM AND OBEYING HIS WILL FOR US, AS WE UNDERSTAND IT.

THERE IS ONLY ONE GOD ---WHO IS KNOWN BY MANY NAMES, Following a particular religion is good and practical as it builds on what has been lived through and learned by our ancestors, IT MUST NOT HOWEVER, CAUSE YOU TO CONDEMN, RIDICULE AND PERSECUTE BELIEVERS OF OTHER FAITHS, WHO ARE ALSO DOING THEIR BEST TO OBEY GOD'S WILL, as they understand it.

OUR TASK IS TO FIND AND SERVE GOD --<u>AND NOT</u>-- TO FORCE OUR BELIEFS ON TO OTHERS. Blind adherence to religious books (obscure passages) or someone's interpretation of their teaching (without conscious thought) can and does lead to **abominations of God's will, Terrorists, Murderers, Secret Societies and so forth. This is clearly demonstrated in our current history and <u>this is the exact opposite of what I believe God wants from us.</u>**

The essence of our journey lies in our honest and heartfelt attempts to serve God. All of my life, I have been a free thinker and have not accepted that Things, Events, Philosophies, Situations, Etc. are as defined by this teacher or that person on their say so. I always first confirm that my own Concepts, Beliefs, Appraisals and Knowledge agree with their opinion and confirm in my mind that what they say is true.

I firmly believe that God gave us a THINKING BRAIN AS A GIFT TO USE and not to ignore our own conscious assessments and deliberations accepting blindly that something is a certain way because IT IS WRITTEN or because someone else says so giving their version or interpretation. Who are the original authors? Is what is written correctly translated and interpreted, -----IS IT RIGHT?

Comfort and inspiration can be found from scripture study as confirmed by millions of holy book students, this works for them and may well work for you, however----

IF IT DOESN'T MAKE SENSE IT COULD BE NONSENSE, WORSE, - IF IT LEADS TO MURDER, MAYHEM & EVIL- IT IS NOT GOD'S WILL

Many things have happened in my life which I found very hard to accept or to understand why they occurred. This caused me to reflect and ponder on life as I have experienced it, the lessons it taught, whether it has any meaning or purpose and to come to terms with what I believe God wants from me, – **the purpose of my life.** The work is on going and the more that I think about my life and my relationship with God the more I believe God reveals to me.

A relationship with a real and meaningful God I have found, is not just useful but is an essential tool to help me manage my life and find purpose in it. Reflection and analysis into the content of my life has convinced me that **God does indeed exist.** Outlined in what follows is my further belief that **God is the source of all that we perceive in our reality,** ---the creator of us and everything that surrounds us.

WHAT HE IS AND HOW AND WHY HE HAS DONE WHAT HE HAS IS THE ESSENCE OF ALL THAT WE COULD EVER KNOW.

Glimpses of the truth concerning God have been shown to all of us (specially the Saints, Scholars and Sages among us and in our ancestors). But because we have no direct face to face contact with our God, it is only possible to view the evidence that our hearts and minds perceive and to interpret this to the best of our ability.

This book is written in an earnest attempt to share with my fellow life travellers some of the insights and revelations that my search and thinking have uncovered for me. **This book is intended to supplement and focus on the most important aspects of what our God requires from us and to strip away confusing elements of the written word.**

<u>It is not intended to replace the written word - but to make it more relevant and useful in our lives.</u> What is presented is my attempt to repay and thank God for the love, help and support God has given me in my life and to establish for me (and hopefully for you) **a believable and accurate reality of our almighty God, that we can use to find Him and accept the help and guidance He offers us.**

I do not proclaim any religious authority or mystical inspiration in what follows. I do not seek disciples or followers, **these thoughts are a free gift** which I share with you in the hope that these will help you on your journey to God. All my life I have been a hard worker and battler trying to make sense of what I have lived through and experienced. **I sincerely hope these thoughts help you.**

Chapter 1

IS THERE A GOD?

Trust and hope in God's guidance and help in your life

<u>IS THERE A GOD?</u> Scholars have pondered this question since time began. What is presented here is the results of my personal search and deliberations.

EVIDENCE FOR A GOD. ------ **Consider the following**

1. **COMPLEXITY OF CREATION.** All living creatures from Conception to Birth, require an exact sequence of events to occur with precise timing to successfully produce one newborn. Millions of cells forming, growing, changing and grouping. Precise chemical changes, the formation of bones, organs, muscles, flesh, limbs, eyes, ears **and most dramatically of all BRAINS.** Scientists tell us that, genes and DNA control all of these processes.

BUT HOW DID THIS ALL COME ABOUT??

In my working life I was a Mechanical Engineer and I soon realised how very difficult it is to create anything where nothing exists, for example, a machine to manufacture a new product, or a system to automatically control a production process. **This requires a huge** amount of thinking, design, deliberation, WILL and perseverance to make it happen.

IT NEVER HAPPENS BY CHANCE. IT REQUIRES INTELLIGENCE, PURPOSE AND WILL TO MAKE IT HAPPEN.

IS IT POSSIBLE THEN THAT HUMAN BEINGS AND LIVING CREATURES, IN ALL THEIR COMPLEXITY, CAME ABOUT BY CHANCE – ACCIDENTALLY WITHOUT INTELLIGENT DESIGN AND PURPOSE ---------------- <u>Very unlikely!</u>

Like all automatic systems the birth sequence does sometimes go astray with birth defects e.g. Down Syndrome children, Siamese twins, too many or too few limbs, other syndromes, retardation, malformation, disease and so forth. This is true for us and animals, birds, fish, reptiles, insects, <u>"ALL LIFE"</u>. **This shows us that, life can not be taken for granted and really what a fantastic miracle it is.**

IT SEEMS INCONCEIVABLE TO ME, THAT LIFE AS WE KNOW IT CAME ABOUT BY CHANCE

The concept that ALL LIFE AND OUR EXISTENCE is the result of various quantities of random raw materials combining by chance is absolutely ridiculous.

GREAT INTELLIGENCE, GREAT DESIGN, PURPOSE, IMMENSE WILL AND LOVE, WENT INTO LIFE CREATION. THIS PROVIDES US WITH STRONG EVIDENCE OF A CREATOR, A SUPREME BEING ----- GOD.

There is no question that we as a species have evolved over the many centuries of time, that we have existed, **BUT AGAIN, WHO designed the system of life that caused this to happen, an evolution system and why is it that <u>all other life</u> on our planet has not evolved to any significant state of thinking, consciousness or awareness. If "Evolution" is the cause of our current development and if we evolved from apes, then why is it that there are still apes around. Further more** why is it that there are species of life that are virtually unchanged from their original form millions of years ago (sharks, crocodiles etc.) How can an evolution system of any sort come into existence of it's own accord? The evolutionists tell us that all life evolves and evolution causes **SURVIVAL OF THE FITTEST** where successful components of our make up develop and continue in successive generations while unsuccessful components gradually disappear.--- **OK but why and arranged by whom ???**

Our thinking ability, consciousness and awareness, I believe is a direct gift from what or Whoever created us,---- OUR GOD----- and this is not given to any other life on our planet. I believe that this entity (God) is revealing more and more of His infinite knowledge to us as we search and research all that we perceive around us. I believe this God watches us with love and interest as we - **LEARN HOW WE REACHED OUR CURRENT REALITY. REFLECT, ON OUR CURRENT STATE AND CHOOSE OUR FUTURE.**

Chance and randomness are not a part of this picture, great intelligence, purpose, determination and love are.

AS WE LEARN AND UNDERSTAND MORE AND MORE, DO WE NOW SEE GOD? OR DO WE ARROGANTLY PROCLAIM OUR INDEPENDENCE FROM HIM, GLORYING IN OUR OWN MAGNIFICENCE?

2. THE REASON FOR LIFE.--- **Are we simply meant to be born, to live and then to die?** If this is so then why should we worry if what we do in our lives is – **WHAT IS RIGHT or WHAT IS WRONG. There is no real and significant reason to do good, instead of evil.**

WHO IN FACT DECIDES, WHAT IS GOOD AND WHAT IS EVIL? If there is no God it is unlikely that anyone will take us to task for what we can get away with.

THE REASON FOR GOODNESS BECOMES NON-EXISTENT.

If we hide our behaviour from our fellow men – WHO WILL KNOW WHETHER WE DO GOOD OR EVIL?

When we consider our lives, is really all we have to look forward to at life's end simply, DEATH and OBLIVION?------ Is there any JUSTICE in our lives or there after?

What is the significance of one person living a lifetime of privilege and wealth, while another lives a lifetime of work and pain, deprivation, servitude, drudgery and everything in between. WHO CARES, except the person's involved and those who form a part of their lives. WITHOUT GOD, why should we live wholesome and productive lives? We could think of ourselves only, care for no one, simply use others to suit our own needs and desires.

WHAT SORT OF A WORLD WOULD THAT BE LIKE TO LIVE IN? OBEDIENCE TO A LOVING GOD WHO COMMANDS US TO LOVE HIM AND OUR FELLOW MEN, PROVIDES US WITH A PURPOSE FOR OUR LIVES (However humble they may be) AND A STANDARD FOR LIVING,---- <u>A TANGIBLE REASON FOR DOING GOOD</u>

3. THE ABILITY TO THINK, DREAM AND REASON. Where did this come from? Is it possible we have this ability by chance- (very unlikely). Is it possible we got our ability to think and reason by evolution, out of nothing (again very unlikely). **Or did some supreme intelligence provide us with this ability and if so, why? We are the only species on this planet, who can think about and ponder our origin, our current state and our future. We can plan where we are going and take action to get there. This ability is not given to any other created life.** What then is the significance of our hopes dreams and aspirations? Do these end when we die? Are we accountable for our actions and if so to whom? (Our fellow men, authorities, who) **Or, are we responsible to our creator---- "OUR GOD"--- Powerful people, Emperors, Kings, Dictators, Presidents, Generals, and others in specific Circumstances,** can

virtually do as they please, **they are in absolute power, who holds them to account?**

WITHOUT GOD,-- in these circumstances --THEY ARE ACCOUNTABLE TO NOBODY, IS THIS FAIR, JUST and in any way desirable? I BELIEVE NOT, I BELIEVE EACH OF US ARE INDIVIDUALLY RESPONSIBLE TO GOD FOR ALL THE CHOICES WE MAKE IN OUR LIVES, and He will hold us accountable, when He decides our place in Eternity. <u>ARE YOU READY TO ANSWER TO GOD FOR THE CHOICES THAT YOU HAVE MADE IN YOUR LIFE?</u>

4. WHAT ABOUT DISABLED, IMPAIRED AND HANDICAPPED PEOPLE, OLD PEOPLE, MENTALLY INCAPABLE AND DISTURBED PEOPLE. Why should we care for and love these? Wouldn't it be practical and pragmatic to simply get rid of them, kill them or similar. This has been tried, by various groups in our history, Eskimos used to leave their old people out in the snow to die, when they were considered to be too old, no longer useful and a burden on the tribe. Should apparently useless and defective peoples lives be terminated? CONSIDER YOURSELF AS BEING ONE IN THIS GROUP, WHAT THEN IS THE SIGNIFICANCE OF YOUR LIFE, (which has been given and entrusted to you by God). DOES ANY OTHER PERSON,------ HAVE THE RIGHT TO TAKE YOUR LIFE? I BELIEVE NOT, FOR ONLY GOD, CAN EVEN OUT THE HUGE VARIATIONS IN HOW WE ARE EQUIPPED AT BIRTH, AND IN WHAT HAPPENS IN OUR LIVES. HE IS, THE ONLY ONE WHO SEES ALL OF THE PICTURE. Man enters God's domain when he makes life and death decisions and should be very careful and indeed prayerful before acting in this area.

<u>GOD MUST DECIDE ON OUR VALUE
AND WORTH, NOT MAN.</u>

5. **SCIENTIFIC DISCOVERY, OUR UNIVERSE** – How immense and marvellous it is with its Galaxies, Star systems, Planets, Black Holes, it's age, vastness, etc. What we have learned and now know about it is overwhelming. Then consider, **OUR WORLD,** The wonder of nature, all living creatures, Man, Animal, Bird, Fish, Insect, Plants, Etc. and **How we all evolved – THIS IS MIND BLOWING STUFF!**-- The intelligence, precision, immensity, majesty and shear awesomeness of all this. Is it possible this came about by chance, a cosmic, accident, most of us struggle to comprehend even small parts of how this came about how it exists now, and how it all works.

   CAN THESE POSSIBLY BE SIMPLE CHANCE OR RANDOM HAPPENINGS? ABSOLUTELY NOT IN MY MIND. What we gradually see is the emergence of our GOD, the creator and source of all that we perceive.

6. **HOW IT ALL WORKS. The precision and exactness associated with the laws and prime values that control Mechanical operations, Electricity, Electronics, Light, Heat, Chemical changes, Hydraulics, Etc., Etc, Etc, who calculated and worked these out? These values were selected by someone, during creation, they could have been entirely different, WHO CHOSE THESE VALUES AND SPECIFIC RELATIONSHIPS?** Each year new discoveries are made, **new to us,** but these things discovered, have existed since the beginning of time. Then **consider the wonder and magnificence of how our bodies and minds work,** natural phenomena in the evolution of ourselves and all of the other creatures that inhabit our planet. **Consider discoveries in engineering, electronics, nuclear energy and all other disciplines.** Where did all this originate, who thought it through and caused it to come into being. The superb design and awesome intelligence behind this. **chance, random, accidental happenings "RUBBISH". ALL OF THIS points out to me the INTELLIGENCE, magnificence, power and immensity of the supreme being who designed and created all of this and is now sharing this knowledge with us.**

THIS COULD NOT HAPPEN BY CHANCE What is also displayed however, is our complete arrogance in somehow believing that magically, we are responsible for all of this wonder around us as we grow to understand it. **The truth being that we are uncovering a minute portion only of our God's infinite knowledge in His creation. There seems to me to be absolutely no possibility that all of this happened by chance or that we caused it to happen.** Scientists proclaim the universe began in a **BIG BANG** and that over millions of years planets formed and life began, crude life which evolution shaped into what we have today virtually a series of chance happenings. I find this inconceivable, to me this would be equivalent to throwing a bucket full of match sticks into the air and have them fall to make a perfect match stick city with buildings and houses perfectly shaped and positioned to each other The only way this could happen is for **someone with will and patience,** to painstakingly take the matches, glue them together, thinking about what and how this city should be and doing what is necessary to make it happen. **Purpose, Design and will,--------- never just chance.**

If there is no God, what are the alternatives? With our short lives, where do we find purpose hope and justice. IS THERE ANYONE THERE TO MAKE THINGS RIGHT FOR US? If you are born a slave, live your life as a slave and then die a slave for a cruel master, ----- **is this just tough luck?**

Our lives are all we know and may seem very long to us as we live them, (few of us will live beyond 100 yr). Again this may seem a long time (our whole life after all). But what is this compared to millions of years, ETERNITY. Our lives are but a mere blip an insignificant instant in ETERNITY, but they, are all important to us, as they are all we have as we live them. What possible HOPE then is there for us ---- without GOD?

ONLY GOD WILL PROVIDE A TRUE MEANING AND PURPOSE FOR OUR EARTHLY LIFE AND - THE PROMISE OF PERFECTION IN OUR SPIRITUAL LIFE, AFTER DEATH, <u>FOR ALL ETERNITY.</u>

Reflection on the above indicates to me the presence of a supreme intelligence and entity that created and caused all of this – **GOD. The awesome power, might and magnificence of this creator is beyond comprehension, but is displayed in all we see around us.**

ALMOST BEYOND BELIEF IS THAT THIS GOD DOES LOVE US, KNOWS EACH AND EVERY ONE OF US AND WILL HELP US IF WE ASK HIM. OH THANK YOU MY GOD.

As an engineer it struck me, IF GOD IS THE CREATOR OF THE UNIVERSE, OF ALL THAT WE PERCEIVE, ------ HOW DID HE DO IT?--------All my working life demanded answers to questions like.

- How does this happen?
- What factors are involved?
- How can we understand, use and manipulate these happenings to suit our purposes?

Geniuses among us past and present people like, Isaac Newton, Archimedes, Leonardo De Vinci, Albert Einstein and **MANY, MANY OTHERS** have uncovered significant answers to part of these questions. **When we reflect on mankind's achievements we see that we imitate little bits only of what God does as our understanding, consciousness, abilities and resources increase, all because of the use of our God given brains – we start to get glimpses of the big picture.**

Just consider that

- We fly in air planes in a huge variety of types and designs.
- We travel in motor cars, huge ships, trains, buses again in a huge variety of types and designs.
- We travel in and explore space (our own solar system mainly at this stage).**Yet our understanding is gradually reaching the limits of our universe - and the minute detail of our existence.**

- We understand (part only at present) Life creation—Things like cell division and replication, DNA, gene purpose and control, body and brain functioning in ourselves and other living species (animal, bird, insect, fish and even plants).

- We understand forces in our world both seen and unseen –Gravity, Magnetism, Electricity, Nuclear Energy, Heat, Light, Infra Red and Radio Waves, Electronic pulse and on and on. We have discovered ways of manipulating and using these to achieve virtual miracles in our world both large and small. The future has almost limitless possibilities for us a direct result of our imagination and research into what happens by using, our God given brains, **the tool that our creator gave us which allows us to understand more and more of His mind and creation.**

We are slowly uncovering the big picture

- We produce miracles in what we design implement and control. Remote control of nearly all functions of TV's, Computers, Electrical appliances, Industrial machines and indeed spacecraft millions of miles away from our planet are amazing to me. Internal control systems designed and built into these devices respond to invisible signals sent to them by us from unbelievable places.

DO WE NOW SEE GOD OR MARVEL IN OUR OWN POWERS?

When we consider the functional requirements of what we want to achieve, how we can implement and control this creation and make it all automatic.**We imitate a little only of what God does.**

We have to use materials at our disposal to make what we imagine. God however can create materials out of nothing **Einstein's famous equation E= MC Squared**, where E is Energy, M is Mass and C is a constant (the speed of light 183000 miles per second multiplied by itself) shows how huge releases of energy are achieved from small amounts of mass and how the reverse energy being converted into mass also applies. For us this truth resulted in the understanding of nuclear energy and the atomic bomb. **This (new to us) understanding has been used by God for countless millions of years in our sun and every star in the sky and results in all the elements we use It reveals to us glimpses of what God has done and can do.** The miracles described in the bible performed by Jesus (God's son) can now in part be duplicated by us with our understanding, Blind people see, Lame people walk, Lepers are cured, Etc. The difference being that Jesus did it without modern equipment, machines, hospitals and so forth. He in most cases did it by remote control with possibly the help of His Father, the Holy Ghost, Angels or the like who were resources available to Him to draw on. The fact that our bodies have been designed to virtually cure themselves (a multitude of overlapping self correcting control systems) and that mostly doctors help us cure ourselves by removing obstacles to the cure, (**shows that understanding and controlling body control systems can make almost anything possible in regard to our bodies**).

Reflection into the above indicates to me the presence of a supreme intelligence an entity that created and caused all of this----**GOD. I believe this God monitors all that happens to each and every one of us and will judge each of us for all of our free will choices. The awesome power, might and magnificence of this creator is beyond our comprehension but is displayed in all that surrounds us.**

Our only hope lies in the promise of God's love for us (which we have not earned but which God provides). Our fundamental and most important task is to establish our relationship with this almighty entity to ensure our salvation, our place in Eternity.

I BELIEVE THAT GOD IS ALL THERE IS. HE IS OUR ONLY HOPE, HE ALWAYS WAS, IS NOW AND ALWAYS WILL BE. THERE IS NOTHING FOR US WITHOUT GOD. This leads us into the next chapter where we consider ---**WHAT CAN OUR GOD BE LIKE?**

Chapter 2

CONCEPT OF A GOD.

Trust and hope in God's guidance and help in your life

What can our God be like? From what has been written, we are told that we are created in God's image and likeness and that God's son became a man like us in all things except sin. Catholic teaching declares that there is only one God but that God's essence is three divine persons **Father, Son and Holy Ghost ---The Trinity.** Nobody has been able to give a satisfactory explanation how the trinity can be one person (our God) and this remains a mystery. It is Catholic doctrine and Catholics accept this in faith. This tends to confuse me but does not detract from my conviction that there is a God, the only explanation for all the wonder and magnificence that we perceive around us further supported by reflecting on the evidence spelt out in the previous chapter.

God caused ---"THE BIG BANG"--- some 14 Billion years ago. He designed and put in place the systems that control all events, forces present and LIFE creation. He is eternal and promises us eternal life with Him if we follow His will, ---- in how we live our lives.

WITH GOD AS OUR CREATOR, I believe that GOD is every where and in everything, the creator of everything. He created our spirits out of His spirit and His spirit is a part of all of His creation.. **It**

follows therefore that He is present in all of His creation and that all of His creation is all a part of Him. This can explain how He knows each and every thing that happens to each and every one of us.

An inkling into the actual mechanics of how all this could happen is revealed in the evolution of computers, their software and electronics etc. All of this is a mystery to most of us and yet simple to those who design, develop and work in this industry. We see that computers keep track of the countless transactions of huge numbers of people and yet each individual receives the permanent record **a statement of each and every transaction he initiated or that affected his account.**

This technology points out possibilities of how God can know each of us and respond to us as individuals. Slowly we start to comprehend small portions of what could be going on. God's actual form and make up will remain unknown to us unless and until God reveals it to us, a distinct possibility as God makes more and more known to us.

As there are millions of us on this planet it may seem that individually we are not important to God. However, the bible and other religious books tell us that this is not so. These books evolved out of our human experience and centuries of our recorded history they tell us that **Each of us is precious and important to God and each of us can build a personal one to one relationship with God, if we try.** Bible stories like" The Good Shepherd" (Luke 15 1-10) Who leaves ninety nine sheep to find the one missing and greatly rejoices when He finds it, and "The Prodigal Son"(Luke 15 11-31) Whose father welcomes him back after this son had squandered his inheritance indicate **God's love for the individual.** God does not need us, but for some inexplicable reason He loves us and wants us to love Him freely by our own choice. I believe this shows that each of us is uniquely precious to God and that

OUR ONLY HOPE FOR SALVATION IS IN THE PROMISE OF GOD'S LOVE, GOD WILL ALWAYS FORGIVE THE SINCERE REPENTER, HE MAY HATE WHAT WE DO, BUT HOPEFULLY,

HE NEVER HATES US. HOPE, TRUST AND FAITH IN GOD ARE WHAT WE NEED TO SUCCESSFULLY MANAGE OUR LIVES.

I believe that God is always ready to help us, forgive us, to give us His soothing healing grace. We however have to be genuinely sorry for what we have done wrong and try to make it right. With our free will we choose what we do, and we (not God), are responsible for what we do.

GOD LOVES US- NOT BECAUSE WE ARE GOOD - BUT SO THAT, WE CAN BECOME GOOD.

He loved us so much that He sent His innocent Son to die most horribly on a cross to save us from our sins. With our human nature and sense of values I find this almost incomprehensible and wonder at this display of God's love of us. With no hope of repaying this love I can only thank God for His goodness. If we changed places with God and as God viewed His creation, I once again marvel at God's patience. The history of mankind is a continuing saga of wars, greed, oppression and injustice **in spite of God's son's example, teachings and love**

WE SEEM NEVER TO LEARN THE LESSON.

THANKFULLY HOWEVER, ITS NOT ALL DOOM & GLOOM AS AMONG US there are many good people obeying God's will and living their lives as they believe God wants them to.

My hope in writing this book is that you its reader will join the ranks of these good people and learn to, cherish and love the God who created you. To search for the purpose and meaning for and in your life and follow God's will for you to enable you to gain the eternal peace and happiness that God promises.

NOTE: In presenting the above I realise that some of this book's readers may not accept the concept that God sent His son into the world **(not accept that Jesus Christ is the son of God).** This however reflects my belief which I share with you. **I trust you will still profit from** my thoughts about God when you reflect on the evidence presented supporting God's existence and the desires and expectations that He has for us.

I trust also that the thoughts presented provide you with adequate material to at least start you thinking about this, the most vital issue in your life and that these ideas will promote your faith and enrich it with views that you may have not previously considered.

Reviewing then, we can perceive God as

- Eternal—Always was is now and always will be.
- Incredibly powerful, all knowing, the creator of all that we perceive in our reality.
- LOVING US, the source and only HOPE for all that we desire.

With Hope, reflection, desire and perseverance, each of us can develop our own unique relationship with our God. ----- He will help, if you seek Him sincerely.

Chapter 3

LET'S TALK ABOUT ATHEISTS.

Trust and hope in God's guidance and help in your life

ATHEISTS DO NOT BELIEVE IN GOD OR IN ANY SUPREME ENTITY!

THEY BELIEVE THAT-- Our universe and all it contains came about purely by chance--- without any plans, intelligent designs and/ or any controlling will or purpose of any sort. A cosmic accident or incident followed by purely chance random happenings.

They believe that our existence and state of being follows scientific speculation, tests, experiments, research, investigations and considered assumptions made by our scientists - as to how we evolved.

The scientific conclusion being that the creation sequence was as follows -

* That our universe started out of nothing in a **Big Bang** (a singularity) with no controlling entity, followed by-- Planet formation from condensing gases and space debris - purely by chance a random occurrence.

- That life started by chance, because—**conditions just happened to be right**, crude life cells started to form and combine in water, which just happened to form from the condensing gases generated in the big bang with the start of planet formation.

- These cells combining in a random sequence of unions which started to form crude living creatures-micro organisms, slugs, worms etc.-which then gradually evolved into more complex creatures – animals,,birds, fish, etc - over millions of years.

- These creatures evolving becoming more and more complex and competing with one another to survive. Then starting to live off one another- preying on one another. **Carnivores and prey type evolution** in all life---- plant, fish, reptile, insect, bird, amphibian, animal. Etc.

- This automatic system of evolution required **Survival of the fittest** which caused the strongest most successful predators to eliminate their opposition by surviving and reproducing. These survivors had the best combinations of abilities –Brains, Strength, Size, Physical attributes –teeth, claws, speed, agility, etc. access to resources and the ability to adapt to constantly changing conditions.

- **That man evolved from these processes becoming the dominant species because of his superior brain and abilities to adapt**

- All this continuing to **Here we are.**

Atheists conclude that this sequence is logical but purely random following no "grand plan" or purposeful design. Nothing was thought about, organised or arranged by anyone --- <u>beforehand.</u> There was no will or purpose form any source, except for that which developed in the evolving life occurring and the combined efforts of the competing species as they survived.

Everything just happened because of the individual contributions of all the creatures involved and the natural processes that occurred and are occurring.

They conclude there is no RIGHT OR WRONG in all of this, ---- it just happens, all chance, random occurrences.

Justice, Fairness, Goodness, Evil, and so forth have no part in this evolution---these are all man made concepts without any absolutes.

These concepts came from us (man) in our evolution, and were defined and introduced by groups and powerful individuals that exist now and existed in our ancestry producing the start and adoption of law and order principals created by us for us in our communal living.

Man invented and promoted the authority of laws and enforcement and this is all that exists. We are only answerable to this authority if we individually choose to be, or <u>if we get caught</u> by man's appointed law enforcement officers.

<u>No higher authority exists,</u> we only need to do what we think is necessary and/or to avoid getting caught and possibly punished – if we break these man made rules.

Birth, Life, Death and Oblivion are "all that there is". We have no spirit, only our bodies and brains, the genetic chance results of the union of our parents and their ancestry. There is--

- No life hereafter, "death" is the permanent and irrevocable end of life.
- There is no compensation, compassion, explanation, regress or relief for what our life consists of as we live it, or there after. ----Our life content is purely the luck of the draw

"BAD LUCK IF IT SUCKS"

- Love, compassion, honesty all high ideals were generated by us as we evolved and our acceptance or otherwise of these concepts are purely our personal choice and conforming with the laws we collectively have generated to suit our shared survival.

- There is therefore no necessity (other than our own beliefs/feelings) to be wholesome and good, all we have to worry about is to avoid getting caught and punished. What we do is purely our own choice and what is imposed on us by law and order community standards and their enforcement.

- There is no purpose or meaning for and in our life, other than what we set for ourselves while we are alive. When we die, who cares, we will only be mourned and missed by those who loved us in our lives. All of our life endeavours, hopes, and dreams end with our death, unless someone else decides to take them up and continue them.

Atheists believe all the glory of and in our world just happened random, chance occurrences. Majestic landscapes, beautiful people, animals, plants, sunrises and sunsets, and so on all just happen.

They believe that the awesome power displayed by various natural events earthquakes, hurricanes, Electrical storms, Tidal waves, Volcanoes, Etc. also just happen, chance results of chance conditions.

That our earth and universe and all they contain just happened and will continue to just happen.

THINK AND REFLECT ON ALL OF THIS—
WHAT DO YOU CONCLUDE?

My thoughts and feelings regarding these beliefs are that they are <u>naive fantasy.</u> I see ordered thought, purpose, reflection and love in our creation and evolution

You the reader of this book have your free will. You will have to make up your own mind on what you choose to believe and use in your life. Again the responsibility for these choices is yours and the consequences of these choices are generated by you.

Think and reflect on these issues, they are the essence of your life ---- and will profoundly determine your fate in the afterlife.

IF IT TURNS OUT - THAT AFTER ALL GOD DOES EXIST - AND WE WILL ENTER AN AFTERLIFE FOR ETERNITY - CONTROLLED BY GOD - WHEN WE DIE.

WHAT A SURPRISE TO ANY ATHEIST !

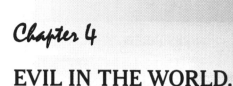

Chapter 4

EVIL IN THE WORLD.

Trust and hope in God's guidance and help in your life

EVIL IN THE WORLD How do we explain it? We are created with **FREE WILL, God wants our love but He wants this to be freely given.** We have a thinking brain at our disposal the most marvellous and wonderful of all of God's gifts to us. How we use what we have however, is for us to choose. We as a species don't, automatically respond to God in a positive loving manner, we in fact frequently reject God and marvel at our own powers and dominance in our world.

ARROGANCE OF ATTITUDE AND PRIDE IN OURSELVES RATHER THAN GOD <u>THIS IS A RECIPE FOR DISASTER.</u>

Catholic scripture talks about **Gods Greatest Creation the archangel Lucifer** the most powerful and perfect of all the angels that God created, so magnificent but with the same major failing common to us human beings – **<u>ARROGANCE AND PRIDE.</u>**

Lucifer believed he did not require the God (who created him) and that he was as powerful as God and therefore that he could be independent from God, ignoring God's will. **God banished Lucifer and his followers to Hell a place of complete separation from God,**

of torment and sorrow. Lucifer is now known by many names, but most commonly, he is called the **DEVIL or SATAN.** The Devil (Satan) **having lost God's love forever will now do all in his power to cause us to lose it also, so that we join him in hell for eternity.**

THE DEVIL IS EVIL INCARNATE AND WANTS OUR DESTRUCTION. HE AND HIS FOLLOWERS (Devils in Hell) ARE THE MAIN SOURCE OF EVIL IN OUR WORLD

It is sublimely easy to forget about God and ignore Him when we are victorious and comfortable in what we do. ----- WE DO THIS AT OUR PERIL!

We are very easy targets for manipulation by the Devil, in this mindset. Evil stems from the Devil, but unfortunately, we have inherent weaknesses in us (in our creation, body, mind and spirit) which make us very vulnerable to the Devil's lies. These characteristics (Impulses) can be readily seen in animal behaviour although they are not sins in their case, WE HAVE FREE WILL - THEY DON'T - we are born with these same impulses but we must control them--- or we sin, for example---

- Predators, chase and kill their prey. Always brutal and sometimes with prolonged cruelty where they play with their prey for an extended period before killing them.

- With pack animals (Wolves, Lions, Dogs, Apes, etc.) The alpha males and females lord their positions over the rest of the pack deliberately tormenting or killing any who may be challengers to their position or who for some reason they dislike.

- Killing by predators purely for the lust of killing, multiple killings not for food, but for pleasure.

- Homosexual and strangely deviant sexual behaviour. Sex at every opportunity, forced if necessary.

- Stealing, or hoarding food from others in the pack who may be starving. Even eating their own newborn offspring.

We humans have the same sorts of impulses but with our higher intellect and free will we can rise above these impulses, OR, we can also wallow in them greatly amplifying, refining and embellishing them with suitable prompting from the Devil.

THESE IMPULSES MUST BE CONTROLLED BY US! OR WE COMMIT SIN AND DO EVIL. – WE IN FACT BECOME PART OF THE EVIL IN OUR WORLD.

NOTE! Serial --- Killers, Rapists, Arsonists, Child Molesters and so forth are all examples of animal behaviour expanded by the Devil's prompting. All these acts by human beings are SINS and require repentance and forgiveness by our God.

We are not animals, God has given us free will for us to choose what we do or don't do. Those who choose to do wrong continuously (influenced and /or controlled by the Devil) almost never change their behaviour voluntarily. Appeals, persuasion, arguments, logic, etc. also seldom work in changing their behaviour.

We have realised this when we live in communities, hence we punish offenders by pain, prison, banishment -------- execution (death) to change or stop their behaviour and to deter others from copying.

To live in communities requires respect for each other and we evolve in our development with laws, customs, traditions, standards, attitudes of respect, individual rights and love.

These cause us to create LAWS and promote our compliance with community standards, WE BECOME CIVILISED and we strive to rise above our primal urges.

OUR FUNDAMENTAL RESPONSIBILITY HOWEVER, IS ALWAYS TO OBEY GOD'S COMMANDS AS WE UNDERSTAND THEM.

EVIL WILL TRIUMPH------ IF WE DO NOT FIGHT IT.

Our apathy, fear, or worse support of Evil always cause it to flourish and only make it harder to stop it, WHICH in most cases is our only hope for survival. No matter what religion you belong to, how strong or weak your beliefs are, whether or not you believe in God at all. Evil must be fought against and stopped or it will grow and overwhelm us.

<u>Only love as commanded by God will
save us and give us eternal life.</u>

EVIL MUST BE FOUGHT AGAINST, OPPOSED AND OVERCOME FOR US TO SURVIVE.

BE WARNED, BE ALERT AND ON YOUR GUARD AGAINST THE DEVIL'S EFFORTS TO SEDUCE AND ENLIST YOU TO DO HIS WORK. THIS IS ALWAYS DISGUISED TO ATTRACT AND ENTICE YOU—NEVER, NEVER, EVER GO ALONG. REMEMBER SIN IS ALWAYS FUN -- ETC. TO START WITH.

<u>EVIL INTENSE & OVERPOWERING --ALWAYS QUICKLY EMERGES—GAINS STRENGTH WITH EVERY SIN COMMITTED -BECOMING ALL BUT UNSTOPPABLE.</u>

<u>BEWARE!----DON'T FORFEIT YOUR SOUL FOR ETERNITY</u>

Chapter 5

SIN

Trust and hope in God's guidance and help in your life

To SIN is to offend God, one commits sin by **knowingly** doing something that they believe to be wrong. I believe that you cannot commit a sin by accident that is by doing something that you think is quite OK. Then being told and convinced that this action is wrong **a sin**, if you now choose to redo it, **IT IS A SIN. Once you believe that something is a wrong thing to do and do it anyway you commit a sin.**

God's basic commands to love Him and to love your fellow man have been extended to huge lengths by various religions and people in authority. Each of us however is responsible for our own soul, and what we do or don't do is for each of us to choose and remains our responsibility.

We will answer to God for our choices. These are our responsibility!

God's basic commands to us were extended by Him in the biblical account of the life of Moses (Exodus 20 1-17) where He gave Moses the 10 Commandments these were basically

1. I am the Lord your God, you shall not have any other God before me.

2. Do not take the name of the Lord your God in Vain.

3. Keep the Sabbath day holy.

4. Honour your father and mother.

5. Do not kill.

6. Do not commit adultery.

7. Do not steal.

8. Do not tell lies about your neighbour.

9. Do not covet your neighbour's wife.

10. Do not covet your neighbour's goods.

Volumes have been written about these commands, their extensions, how to interpret the detail of what they mean, whether they apply in times of war and so forth.

THIS IS OF VITAL CONCERN TO US AND INVOLVES US IN MORAL DECISIONS THAT WE HAVE TO MAKE FOR OURSELVES ---- AND FOR WHICH WE WILL BE JUDGED BY GOD.

The Ten Commandments are an extension of God's basic instructions to love Him and our fellow men. They in no way conflict with His basic instructions to us, how we extend these instructions further and apply them to our lives is for us to ponder, think about, pray and establish.

Do not gloss over this lightly -- WE ARE RESPONSIBLE FOR OUR ACTIONS -- and we must take the time and make the effort to think this through for ourselves. This is where we can get huge help by following an established religion. One whose followers have agonised over, prayed and lived through the hardships and drama of this religion's evolution. We build on what has been lived through and learned.

WE MUST USE OUR FREE WILL TO CHOOSE TO DO, WHAT WE BELIEVE GOD WANTS FROM US AND FIGHT OFF THE DEVIL'S ATTEMPTS TO TEMPT US TO DO OTHERWISE.

WE HAVE TO CHOOSE, GOD WON'T DO IT FOR US

God wants us to love Him and be good. Like parents watching their child in a competition God can only encourage, equip, instruct and support. The child (us) has to compete, the child's efforts determine success or failure, the Devil will do all in his power to promote our failure, to cause us to sin, to lose our souls for eternity and join him in hell. Once again we choose what we do or don't do, this is our responsibility. Don't blame others for the choices that you make.

Similarly, we are warned about the **seven deadly sins, to which man is most susceptible.**

PRIDE—COVETOUSNESS—LUST—ANGER—GLUTTONY—ENVY—SLOTH.

Once again volumes have been written about these sins and these again involve moral judgements for which we are responsible and that we must make for ourselves.

All of the above (seven deadly sins) only become sins when they are indulged in, in excess. Excesses in almost any form of human behaviour can become sinful. - Moderation in everything is very good advice, but is difficult to achieve.

Overindulgence in almost anything is sinful, eating-**gluttony,** alcohol-**addiction,** drugs-**addiction,** gambling-**addiction,** exercise and diet- **addiction (anorexia),** rest- **sloth, laziness** and so on. **When we become addicted we virtually put ourselves into the power of the**

devil. The road back is always extremely difficult and without God's help impossible. However, if you don't start you won't have to stop.

AVOIDANCE & NON-INDULGENCE IS FAR EASIER THAN COMING BACK FROM ADDICTION!------ Don't start and you won't have to stop.

As previously stated God wants us to be happy, He does not want long suffering, austere, deprived people for His followers.--- **But our danger is the Devil, our own weakness and tendency to over indulge** --- Sin usually starts out as fun, exciting, humorous, fulfilling, dangerous, etc.----But very rapidly degenerates from there.

The Devil is the master of lies, seduction, deception and manipulation; he desperately wants us to sin against God so that like him we will lose our souls and any possibility of HEAVEN.

Sin is EVIL and EVIL must be fought against whenever we encounter it. The saving of our souls depends on this. – Doing nothing just hoping that the evil will go away is not **an option.**

We must FIGHT, FIGHT, FIGHT, FIGHT -- and – FIGHT, TO SAVE OUR SOUL.

The length of our earthly life in time is an insignificant speck, one second when compared with our eternal fife, **but is all important to each of us in determining our place in eternity. Our life is our test to gain Heaven and no one else can do it for us.**

All of us will commit some sins in our lives but because of the sacrifice of Jesus (God's son) we can be forgiven so long as we are genuinely sorry for what we have done wrong, try to stop any repeat of our sin and if possible try to make amends .

Never however lose sight of THE ENORMITY AND ABSOLUTE HORROR OF THE LOSS OF YOUR SOUL, CONDEMNED TO HELL FOR ETERNITY.

This HORROR, can only be glimpsed at WE MUST REALISE ABSOLUTELY THAT THERE IS NOTHING MORE IMPORTANT IN OUR LIVES THAN TO SAVE OUR SOUL.

In the Lords Prayer Jesus asks His Father **"Lead us not into temptation, But deliver us from evil"** and this shows **how dangerous it is to be tempted.** If you have sinned always avoid the circumstances that caused you to do this and / or be doubly on your guard to avoid re offending. **Sin is very very easy,** it often starts out being fun, a dare, - **join in with the "IN CROWD".**

- A friend offers you a pill, "Take this it will make you feel great" he tells you and it does the 1st.time you take it, and the next, and the next, etc. until you can't do without it. **The start of drug addiction.**

- You are in a trusted position at work, no one will notice you taking some money for yourself, so you take some, then some more, then some more, etc. **Your now into stealing.**

- Your friends don't like Wogs, Slopes, Boongs, Nigger's, Kikes, or any other derogatory name they give to foreigners or minorities in our country, they don't associate with them, rubbish them at every opportunity and expect you to do the same if you want their friendship. "Your not one of them, your all right mate "they tell you" its them who are impostors, scum, evil, less than any of us" **They tempt you into race prejudice, persecuting minorities, or those who are different? Don't join them. Love as commanded by God is the required action**

- Sex is one of the strongest urges that we have, overindulgence and deviant sex is sinful. Because it is a powerful motivator the devil uses it to great effect to corrupt and seduce us. The main purpose of sex is for us to reproduce (carry on our species) however, because of the pleasure and joy of the act, it often becomes an end in itself done purely for pleasure's sake and children are an unwanted consequence of it. If the birth of children is prevented (contraception) and sex is carried out purely for pleasure then this is considered by some to be sinful.---- **Each of us need to make up our own minds about this, --- it is important to not take this lightly and to pray and consult God about this before you make up your mind.** It is not a clear cut issue and it is a mistake to lightly accept current convention or someone else's say so, think it through for yourself and FOCUS ON what you believe to be GOD'S WISHES FOR YOU, IN YOUR DELIBERATIONS. Be honest with yourself and decide on what you believe God wants from you. Deviant sex is sinful. The devil gleefully tempts us, inviting us into the world of pornography viewing drawings, pictures, movie s, videos, live demonstrations, etc. joining in various groups or clubs, reading books and so forth. Once again the start down this road is often fun, exciting, daring, etc. but soon leads to perversion, depravity, rapes, murders, child molestation, service to the devil and loss of our soul. **True love and respect for your partner, Family love and wholesomeness soon disappear -**

BEWARE, DON'T BE DECEIVED OR SEDUCED, --- YOUR SOUL IS AT RISK.

Sin never appears EVIL or UGLY in our early indulgence, <u>but this blunts and conditions us to it's monstrous evil, depravity, cruelty, perversion and addiction--- which soon appear.</u>

This is not new, it has occurred time and time again through our history. The devil was, is and will be successful in corrupting and perverting those of us who do not fight him.

Ask for God's help and fight, fight, fight to save your soul. DON'T EVER GIVE IN BECAUSE IT'S TOO HARD, DIFFICULT, STRANGE, UNPOPULAR, WHATEVER,

NEVER RISK YOUR SOUL, YOUR CHANCE AT HAPPINESS FOR ETERNITY

The devil loves the destruction of innocence, hence sins involving children delight him and greatly sadden God. Jesus said in regard to children (Luke 17 2-3) "He would be better off thrown into the sea with a millstone around his neck than giving scandal to one of these little ones".

Again, (Mark 10 13-15) "Let the children come unto me and do not hinder them. It is to just such as these that the kingdom of heaven belongs".GOD LOVES INNOCENCE & TRUST. ---

<u>Destroy this at your peril.</u>

DON'T MAKE IT EASY FOR THE DEVIL BY SINNING, SMALL SINS QUICKLY BECOME LARGE SINS AND THE DEVIL BECOMES MORE AND MORE POWERFUL IN YOUR LIFE WITH EVERY SIN YOU COMMIT.

WITHOUT EXTREME CARE ---YOU WILL BE OVERWHELMED. YOUR SOUL IS AT STAKE AND YOU RISK LOSING YOUR SOUL FOR ETERNITY.

Chapter 6

RELIGION

Trust and hope in God's guidance and help in your life.

God has given us an instinct to suspect His existence and to seek Him. You have only to look at all the religions in the world, Indigenous Tales, Mythologies, Sun worshippers, Moon worshippers, followers of all sorts of imagined gods, virtually religions for every occasion, both in our past and in our present day. **Which are real and which are imagined (man created)?**

Through out our evolution, specially in our early days, **GOD** appears to have directly contacted and inspired chosen ones amongst us, to help guide us to Him. **These are the prophets, sages, saints, etc. among us. These contacts I believe caused the worlds major religions to come into existence CHRISTIANITY, ISLAM, JUDAISM -----and so forth.**

We as a group however, seem to turn away from God when we get comfortable, feel superior, and our arrogance takes over. **Pride in our knowledge and achievements, with the prompting of the devil, generates the arrogance that separates us from God. I believe that there is only one God, one Creator of all that forms our reality and consciousness. His teaching is consistent and is summed up in two fundamental commands.**

1. **TO LOVE THE LORD YOUR GOD WITH YOUR WHOLE HEART AND SOUL AND ALL YOUR STRENGTH AND ALL YOUR MIND.**

2. **TO LOVE YOUR FELLOW MAN AS YOUR SELF** (do only unto him as you would do to yourself)

All the major religions assert the above. Men however, add a million and one rules, assertions and interpretations that muddle, confuse and detract from God's commands to us, further----**THE DEVIL'S LIES, LIES, LIES, LIES --TWIST AND DISTORT WHAT GOD WANTS FROM US. --- DON'T BE DECEIVED!** I believe the world's greatest teachers were inspired by God at appropriate times to help men find their way to God and they were responsible for starting the major religions producing their religious books -

Teachers	Book	Religion
Abraham, Moses, Solomon, David Etc.	The Torah	Jewish religion.
Buddha	Buddhist teachings	Buddhists
Mohammed	The Koran	Moslem religion. ISLAM.
Jesus (God's son), Peter, Paul,(His apostles.)		
Saints like Francis of Assisi, Patrick,		
Martin Luther,		
All Christian teachers.	The Bible	Christianity

Many more books, teachers and religions could be added to this list. **The important truth is that none of us really know, comprehend, or fully appreciate our God.** We get insights, glimpses and imagine concepts of our infinite, all powerful and mighty God, but most of us still doubt and are unsure **of His existence and His actual reality in our lives.**

What God looks for in us is Faith and of fundamental importance is our response to God in how we live our lives. Do we follow his commands and His son's example? **I completely fail to understand WHY IS IT THAT EVEN IN CHRISTIAN RELIGIONS (who have the same source and teacher) FOLLOWERS SOMETIMES FIGHT TO**

THE DEATH OVER DETAILS OF DOCTRINE ACCUSING EACH OTHER OF HERESY AND PUT THEM TO DEATH. WE REFUSE TO EVEN CONSIDER ANY ALTERNATIVE TO OUR BELIEFS.

THIS SINS AGAINST GOD'S BASIC COMMANDS. This can not possibly serve our God, we virtually ignore His wishes and the stupidity and tragedy of doing this, is that it is usually done MISS GUIDE-IDLY for God and in His name.

Similarilly non Christian religions opposed Christianity and fought numerous wars to the death, declaring Christians UNBELIEVERS to be killed. Furthermore like Christians they fought to the death against each other on various versions of their own beliefs.

I BELIEVE THE DEVIL'S LIES TO US, COUPLED WITH OUR ARROGANCE AND WEAKNESS CAUSES THESE ABOMINATIONS - AND THAT THIS IS A COMPLETE CONTRADICTION OF WHAT GOD WANTS FROM US.- THIS IS <u>RELIGION GONE CRAZY</u> - TWISTED AND USED BY THE DEVIL TO DAMN US.

Religion, as a formal recognition of God, what He wants from us, and our sincere and heartfelt desire to love Him and live according to His will, is wholesome and good for us and will lead us to Him. Following our religion with our fellow men in groups (communities) with standards of behaviour developed to serve God and all humanity I believe pleases God. Once again the dangers of a formal religion lies in its leaders speaking their ideas and interpretations of God's will as they think **BUT contrary to what God actually wants from us.**

When told - IT IS WRITTEN AND THIS MEANS THAT YOU DO - is virtually only an interpretation of what is written by those who tell us. – DON'T SWITCH OFF YOUR THINKING BRAIN (GOD'S GIFT TO YOU). If certain issues are not clear to you ALWAYS PRAY FOR GOD'S HELP IN DECIDING WHAT YOU WILL DO. <u>Your responsibility is always directly to God and not to any man.</u> Blind observance and obedience to a misguided religious instruction results in abominations of God's will for us producing bigots, terrorists, suicide bombers and so forth.

ALWAYS THINK ABOUT WHAT GOD WANTS FROM YOU other's proclamations and book interpretations of God's word may not be correct. We can learn from sincere, honest, devout, studious, religious leaders however, **we not they, are responsible to God, for what we do in our lives.** RELIGION MUST ALWAYS BE AN AID TO SERVING GOD & NEVER AN END IN ITSELF, GOD WANTS US TO LOVE HIM AND OUR FELLOW MAN.

RELIGION MUST SUPPORT THIS FOR
IT TO BE OF ANY USE TO US.

A further complication in our use of religion is that if we believe strongly in a particular religion. The Devil (the master manipulator, liar, corrupter and seeker of our downfall) can twist, distort and use our faith against us. This is clearly demonstrated by considering just 3 of the world's major religions, Christianity, Islam and Judaism. In our recorded history we find members of each fighting and killing members of the other faith declaring them "Unbelievers" deserving of death Not only that they kill members of there own faith if their beliefs are not identical in every detail to various power groups in their religion.

How ridiculous is this, when virtually each group believe in the same one and only God who demands love for Him and our fellow men.

This clearly shows the Devil's ability to manipulate, twist and pervert a devout person's belief. God commands us to love our fellow man as ourselves, how can this convert to killing him for his concept of God and understanding of God's will, worse still, to believe that this is done for God, and in His name.

RELIGION IS ONE OF THE DEVIL'S FAVOURITE
MEANS OF CAUSING MAN TO DO UNTOLD EVIL
FOR HIM AGAINST US (MAN'S FELLOW MAN).

He does this by LYING to us and using all our weaknesses against us. His greatest successes occur when he enlists us to do his EVIL work for him. I believe the Devil convinced Adolph Hitler that the Germans were the master race and that all others should serve them before the second world war and demonstrated the harm that these ideas and actions taken caused the rest of us.

There are many more examples in our history.

- The forced Christian conversion of the natives of South America by the Spanish (Conquistadors) they murdered thousands, impaling them on stakes and committing all sorts of atrocities to try to force their brand of Christianity on them.

- The Crusades by Christians to free the Holy Land in medieval times. Sacking towns, looting, raping and murdering.

- Corrupt Popes, Bishops and Clergy who gained power and wealth by using religion and people's faith to manipulate, exploit and steal money from believers.

- The Ku Klux Klan (who called themselves Christians) who brutally suppressed the Negro and Jew in the deep south of America by persecution, injustice and murder.

- Medieval Inquisitions, Trials, Persecutions and Executions of so called Heretics, Witches and others.

- Exclusive Secret Societies in All major religions that murder and commit atrocities.

- There are many more that use **religion misguided,** for **Evil,** rather than as a means to **help man find God. THE OBSCENITY OF THEIR ACTIONS BEING THAT THEY DO IT FOR GOD AND IN HIS NAME.**

My belief is that we can learn from all religions and religious teachers as long as their teachings reflect God's fundamental commands to us -**To love God first and to love our fellow men**

THIS IS AN ABSOLUTE.

Sincere and devout people have lived in every age, their struggles against Evil and the lessons that they learned in their lives can surely provide insights and knowledge that we can learn from and apply in our lives. **Once again God has given us a thinking brain and we are responsible for our actions. Our Evil actions can NOT be justified by anything we read or by anything anyone else tells us. I believe what God wants from us is a loving free spirit, intent on loving Him (our God), not a pedantic rigorous follower of rules and instructions.** I personally find that intense reading of religious books (Bible, Koran, Etc.) does not help me and indeed I find various contradictions in the passages I read.

Many faithful and devout people believe that these books are the inspired word of God and would not question any part of what is written I have my doubts about this, who published what from what source and when. EACH OF US MUST HOWEVER, CHOOSE FOR OURSELVES WHAT WE BELIEVE AND OUR PATH TO GOD! I believe what is written has to make sense and **must always agree with God's basic commands to us TO LOVE HIM AND OUR FELLOW MAN. Are these translations accurate? I further believe that our all loving God will never reject any of His creation who seek Him with an honest and sincere spirit and who follow His will as they understand it to the best of their ability. <u>Learn from the books by all means, but do not follow them blindly or blindly accept an other's interpretations of what they mean.</u>** I do believe most of what is written indeed came from God, however, man with perhaps the Devil's prompting has contaminated what is written resulting in obscenities like those tabulated above and much more.

- Terrorist groups, suicide bombers, anti God actions and willing workers for the Devil.

- Secret organisations (IRA, Royal order of Plymouth Brethren, Masons, Islamic Jihad, Hammas, etc.) whose actions are very far from God's will.

- Any person or group that deliberately causes harm and injury to innocent people are doing the Devil's work,"the end justifies the means" is no excuse for sins against God.

Jesus Christ (God's son) laid down His life for us, taught us and gave us an example of how to accept and obey God's will as we live our lives. Let Jesus be our guide, any action contrary to His example and teaching, does not come from God.

I am a practising Catholic mainly because I was raised and educated in Catholic schools and because my parents were Catholic. I do not in any way believe this is the only way, or even that this is the best way to find God. It feels comfortable and right for me and in spite of searching, I have **not found** a religion which suits me better, (one that my thinking ability chooses as superior).

It is however, for each of us to find God in our own lives, what works for me may not work for you, but you will find God if you seek Him with a sincere and open heart. A religion can help us dramatically as these have evolved over centuries of human experience, our search is probably a mirror of millions of people before us and we can learn from them. Following an organised religion which we choose (bearing in mind God's Fundamental commands to us) can profit us by building on what others have lived through, thought about and recorded before us. We however must choose the detail of what we do or don't do, what in fact we comply with, <u>the essence of our moral framework,</u>

WHAT WE BELIEVE GOD WANTS FROM US.

Shared belief in God, with set standards of behaviour, love and support for each other and formal religious doctrine all help in our journey to God.

EACH OF US HOWEVER, MUST SEARCH FOR, FIND GOD AND ACCEPT HIM FOR OURSELVES. THIS IS THE MOST IMPORTANT GOAL AND THE FUNDAMENTAL PURPOSE OF OUR LIVES.

Chapter 7

SO WHAT IS GOD LIKE & WHAT IS MY RELATIONSHIP WITH HIM?

Trust and hope in God's guidance and help in your life

When we acknowledge that God is our creator and the creator of our universe (our reality) we can with a little further thought realise that

GOD IS IMMENSELY POWERFUL, ALL KNOWING and INFINITE. Thinking about God's creation with awe and wonder, we can reflect and consider --

- **The immensity of the universe and how wondrous it is.** Light travels at 183 000 miles per second and our nearest star is many light years (distance travelled by light in one year) away from us. There are billions of solar systems (Star / planet systems) in our universe at distances almost beyond comprehension. Each solar system has a star at its centre, **our solar system has our sun each star produces a constant series of massive nuclear explosions**, producing heat and light, which continue for millions of years. The star then grows to become a red giant as it's nuclear fuel runs out, eliminating all life on planets close enough to be effected, **scientists predict this will happen with our sun/earth system approx. 500 000 000 years from now, the process then** culminates in a super nova (a massive explosion) causing the star to finally collapses into itself, the end of the star and <u>with our sun - our solar system - our earth and all of us.</u>

- This planet we inhabit shows us incredible displays of energy in volcanic eruptions, earthquakes, cyclones, tidal waves and so forth. If God is indeed the creator of all of this, His power is immense. We are learning more and more about our universe and our world. Yet all we know and have learned is only a minuscule though growing part of God's revealed knowledge to us. He designed and caused all of this to come into being. He now monitors and controls all that happens. He caused "The Big Bang" the start of our universe (some 14 billion years ago) and was there long before this happened. He will still be there if and when it ends.

- The complexity of God's creation, our scientists have studied, thought intensely about, tested, modelled and finally understood some only of the way things work in our reality, they are very far from knowing it all. Just consider the complexity, magnificent design and wonder of

    - Our bodies (Structure, Bones, Organs, Cells, Blood, Chemistry, Genes, Etc)

    - Our minds (Structure, Memory, Reasoning, Conscious and Sub conscious thought, imagination, Etc) and how we use these to increase our understanding of everything.

    - Our fellow creatures (Animals, Birds, Fish, Insects, Etc)

    - Physical Laws and Forces (Electricity, Magnetism, Nuclear Energy, Heat, Light, Sound,) we learn about Quantum Mechanics, String Theory and new ways of understanding how our universe works and how we can manipulate and use this knowledge to serve our own purposes.

DO WE NOW SEE GOD OR DO WE GLORY
IN OUR MAGNIFICENCE?

New discoveries are made almost daily clearly demonstrating that we don't know it all. **IN FACT WE ARE ONLY UNCOVERING, NEW TO US, ASPECTS OF OUR CREATOR'S INFINITE KNOWLEDGE.**

The precision, intricacy and wonder of what we are learning and **the unbelievable intelligence of it all – is truly awe inspiring and provides clear evidence of a supreme creator --- our God.** This God is allowing us to uncover and understand some only of the aspects of his mind. Chance and randomness have no part in this. **WILL, PURPOSE & LOVE DO!** Again some of us are tempted to believe that we know it all. Through out our history, those at the forefront of current knowledge always think that they are very smart and **VIRTUALLY KNOW IT ALL**, only to find that further **PURSUIT OF KNOWLEDGE** invariably uncovers radical **NEW DISCOVERIES which tend to dwarf into the very ordinary what was known previously at that particular stage of development.**

This trend with our current research and pursuit of knowledge is causing increasingly RAPID AND UNCOMFORTABLE CHANGES IN ALL OF OUR LIVES. On reflection this demonstrates to me how little we know, when we compare ourselves to GOD our creator, (the designer and the source of all the knowledge we are uncovering). We as it were get a glimpse of almost limitless possibilities. To think that somehow we are responsible for all this wonder as we start to understand it and that we know it all -- **IS STUPID and ABSOLUTE ARROGANCE – Lucifer (the Devil) did exactly this and suffered the consequences!**

God reveals His mind to us and suddenly we think that we know it all and that we don't need God. **What a trap for young players and massive opportunity for the Devil to manipulate us.**

GOD IS THE INVENTOR, DESIGNER AND CREATOR OF ALL THAT FORMS OUR REALITY. HE TRULY IS ---- ALL, THAT THERE IS.

What then is my relationship with my God? It is appropriate now to review chapter 2 Concept of a God., the bible tells us that we are created in God's likeness, so when we think of God we can imagine Him this way although with infinite power, knowledge and love.

- **God has infinite power and magnificence**, so why should He love us? Our insignificance in this overall creation makes it seem as though we could not possibly count. This however is contradicted in the books of every significant religion. **God's message to those He has contacted is always one of love and mercy for each and every one of us, we can form a one to one relationship with God, the magnificent, the almighty, what an awe inspiring thought (mind blowing).** How it all works is unknown to me, that it works I have experienced, leaving me in awe of God, humble, but very grateful to God for His love of me.

- **God is just.** He cares what we do, and how our actions effect our fellow men. He knows exactly what we do and why we do it. **God will be our judge, when we die, we have FREE WILL in our earthly lives. God is loving but righteous, dare we offend this immense power. How foolhardy, reckless and arrogant we are, when we do.**

Because we have FREE WILL (given to us by God) we can shut Him out, refuse to acknowledge Him, consider ourselves more important than God. This will separate us from God, we may not do this in an evil way like exploiting or persecuting our fellow men or committing other sins. The result however is the same! WE WILL CUT OURSELVES OFF FROM THE ONLY LIFELINE THAT WILL SATISFY ALL OF OUR NEEDS.

HOW STUPID IS THIS?

I believe the major pain of Hell is absolute and complete separation from God. God is the only source of satisfaction for all of our needs. Every need and desire we have is satisfied by God if we succeed in our earthly life trials and we gain Heaven.

If you ever loved someone intensely and lost that person forever, their death and your separation from them would cause you pain and loss. But what you felt would be tiny compared with what you would feel-if you lost Gods love.

THE ENORMITY, COMPLETE DEVASTATION AND IMMENSITY OF THAT LOSS CAN ONLY BE GLIMPSED AT --- IN OUR EARTHLY EXPERIENCE.

The Devil's hatred and jealously of us is a direct result of his loss of God's love. The Devil wants us to join him in his misery, completely cut of from the peace and happiness that God's love gives us.

We form and develop our relationship with God by opening ourselves to Him, choosing Him with our free will, loving Him intensely, respecting Him, sharing with Him all our hopes, dreams and aspirations seeking His guidance and help in all our endeavours and following His instructions to us, which are again

TO LOVE THE LORD YOUR GOD WITH YOUR WHOLE HEART AND SOUL, WITH ALL YOUR STRENGTH AND WITH ALL YOUR MIND and TO LOVE YOUR NEIGHBOUR AS YOURSELF.

This is the essence of what God wants from us. Ancient scriptures, scrolls, books, gospels, Etc. are claimed by some to be the word of God, some may be, others definitely are not, with God's help we will be able to distinguish between them. We can learn a great deal from other's writings and they can help our spiritual growth. Never however, accept them blindly or worse, accept someone's interpretation of what they mean,

PRAY TO GOD TO GUIDE YOU CLEARLY.

Personally I am confused by too many instructions and so called versions of God's words to us. I try to keep it simple and do my best to stick with God's fundamental instructions to us (above). I always test what is written in the light of these instructions and my own thinking. I always ask for God's help to guide me and this has led me to **my current relationship with God -- which is offered by God to ALL OF US. In God's relationship with me I believe that –**

- **God loves me no matter what "UNCONDITIONAL LOVE".** Why, I don't know but I trust in my heart that He does and count on His love, guidance and protection.
- He loves me all the time. 24 hrs. Per day, every day of my life.
- He loves me no matter how bad I have been, He will no doubt hate the bad things that I have done, but He never hates me. **He is always ready to forgive me when I am <u>truly sorry</u> for what I have done wrong ---.GOD'S LOVE IS A CONSTANT THAT I CAN COUNT ON.**
- He loves me no matter how bad I feel about myself. – **<u>His love enables me to</u> <u>become good and feel good about myself.</u>**
- He will guide, comfort and support me when I have a problem or situation I can't face.
- He is always on my side and always there for me.
- He helps me get the things I desire when I ask Him sincerely (when they are good for me).
- He is my unconditional friend and I call Him **Jesus.**

This loving relationship with God is offered to each and every one of us. We however, must choose to take it and work to develop it. When faced with life's problems God is our greatest resource. WHY then do we cut ourselves off from God? The devil has a massive victory when he persuades us with lies to cut ourselves off from God.

THE DEVIL RUBBISHES THE ABOVE AND TRIES TO CONVINCE US THAT GOD

- Causes our problems.

- Does not care about us and is completely indifferent to our plight, our worries, and our prayers.

- Enjoys and amuses Himself by callously exposing us to all sorts of difficulties.

- **Does NOT LOVE US,---does not care,---that we are of no consequence and unimportant to Him.**

Don't be deceived, <u>THESE ARE LIES,</u> ---- THAT THE DEVIL WANTS US TO BELIEVE.

GOD DOES LOVE US, He wants only good for us and wants us to succeed in all that we do.

Think about the politics (Power play involved) God is powerful and so is the devil, infinitely more powerful than any of us. Without God's help and protection we would be powerless and completely vulnerable to manipulation by the devil.

God is our only hope. We desperately need God, God does not need us, we are His creation to do with as He pleases, and if He wanted our downfall--- He could destroy us instantly. The fact that God does not, that he gives us a free will to live our lives as we choose and waits patiently and hopefully for us to choose Him demonstrates that God does indeed love us. His love is promised to us in all major religious books.

HIS LOVE IS HIS COMMITMENT TO US <u>AND IS OUR ONLY HOPE.</u>

So why would it ever be smart to cut ourselves off from God's love, OUR ONLY LIFELINE. Life is not meant to be easy. No matter

who you talk to, everyone has problems; no body has a free ride. The problems are different for each of us and each of us has different abilities, talents, and resources at our disposal to cope with our problems. How we cope and use what we have is our choice. We have been designed to succeed and be happy, we can however choose otherwise. No matter how bad our problems are we can always find people whose problems are worse than ours. So what, gives us the right to----

- Whine, Moan and complain about our problems.
- Feel so very sorry for ourselves.
- Get angry and rebellious with God blaming Him for our distress and all the problems in the world.

All of us are in the same boat, **God has given us so much, <u>it is our duty to be happy</u>,** we don't have to work at it, **we need to accept what we have been given (entrusted to us) and play the cards we have been dealt, (our lot in life).** ------God will help us on our way if we trust in Him and ask for His help.

BEWARE THE DEADLY TRAP OF SELF PITY, it is very easy for the devil to manipulate us when we feel sorry for ourselves, believe we are hard done by because we don't have something someone else has, or, -- we carry a burden or handicap others are free from.

Happiness is not earned it is given to us to accept and be happy. We are like ungrateful children who destroy the toys they are given because they are not what they wanted, when we do not accept with love and gratitude, what we have been given.

Always focus on our gifts not other peoples Our earthly lives are so short (100 years or less for most of us) How can this compare to eternity and the promise we have from God, **that we will have eternal happiness with God, if we obey His will for us.**

We owe it to ourselves and to God to be happy with what we have in this life, making the most of all our opportunities.

There is nothing to stop us striving mightily for what we want in our lives, don't however ever blame God for what you don't achieve or have in this life. **We are designed to succeed and be happy, if we choose otherwise, whose fault is that?**

Reviewing then, God is all powerful, magnificent and the source of all that we could ever hope for. He loves us more than we could ever imagine and wants only the very best for us.

In spite of this our lot in life may be pain, suffering and less than any expectation we could have. Don't lose hope however, trust and ask God to help you

FAITH in God's goodness and love will help us through <u>all of our earthly trials</u> and <u>these trials will fade into insignificance when we share ETERNITY with God</u>.

God promises us complete happiness with Him for eternity, when our trials here are over; if we abide by His will for us.

FAITH IN THIS TRUTH WILL GIVE US THE HOPE TO SEE LIFE THROUGH.

Chapter 8

GOD IN OUR LIVES

Trust and hope in God's guidance and help in your life

As we live our lives most of us automatically and routinely attend to family, work, social and other matters, we more or less coast through our lives in a blur of activity.

BUT - WE SHOULD TAKE STOCK AND WONDER WHAT OUR LIFE IS ALL ABOUT? WHY WE'RE HERE AND WHERE WE'RE GOING AS OUR LIFE IS TIMING OUT. WE CAN CLAIM WE'RE FAR TOO BUSY TRYING HARD TO REACH OUR GOAL. WE SHOULD HOWEVER STOP AND REALISE - <u>THE IMPORTANCE OF OUR SOUL.</u>

Current technology, scientific investigation, applied research, what we have collectively learned and discovered about—Origin of life, anthropology, creation and evolution, ----all tend to dismiss any belief that----**A God created us and our world.**

We've been taught that everything that exists started in a **Cosmic Big Bang** followed by planet formation from space debris which created our planet and all that exists in our universe. Then that life started, simple basic life began and became more and more complex evolving finally to the emergence of our species. **Where is God in all of this?**

With more than seven billion of us living on our planet is it even remotely possible to believe that a God exists, a God who knows each of us individually, who knows the detail of what is happening in our lives and forces involved, a God who can actually guide and help us in our life trials and personal endeavours.

Pragmatically we could conclude that —" **WE ARE ON OUR OWN**".

Still we marvel at,-- the glory, beauty, majesty and power of what we see and experience in our world—**Sunrise and Set, Flowers, Mountains, Oceans, Rivers, Volcanoes, Hurricanes, Earthquakes, Tsunamis,--- and so forth.**

We wonder at-- the precision, magnificent design, complexity and composition of all life, Man, Animal, Plants, etc on our planet and the awesome vastness of our cosmic universe and all it contains.

Could a God be possible? –"YES, YES",-- not only possible but loving us and leading us back to Him. Re read chapters 1 and 2 and stop, think and reflect on what they contain.

Belief in God as our creator and that He is the creator and source of all that we perceive generates joy in our lives and provides us with a framework and set of tangible standards that we can live by.

Following His instructions to us as reported and passed on to us (Bible, Koran, Torah, etc.) and opening ourselves to direct messages we receive from Him, fulfils our obligation and desire to abide by His will for us. These standards then provide the concept of goodness as opposed to evil and give us a tangible reason for being and doing good. The incredible volume of information that we have had passed on to us from our ancestors concerning God, His make up, His commands to us, and so forth all point out His existence. It is very unlikely that the countless millions of our ancestors--- have all been deceived.

The reason therefore why we should believe in God is because this is THE ACTUAL REALITY OF OUR LIVES and the TRUTH OF OUR EXISTENCE and we are only recognising and acknowledging this fact when we believe in God.

It is however very difficult to understand and make sense of the huge variations in all of our lives and their relative contents. Some of us have so much wealth, health, good luck and abundant good fortune, while others endure poverty, sickness, deprivation, bad luck and miss fortune WHY?

Huge variations both positive and negative occur in ALL of our lives without any apparent reason, cause, explanation or sense of WHY this happens. The apparent worthiness or otherwise of the people involved and their life content is also very confusing. Bad things happen to good people and visa versa. **Is there any justice in all of this, where is God and why does He not intervene as all this happens? Non of us knows God's mind and we become presumptuous and self serving if we think we know best and that we can advise God on what is right and wrong in the world and what should happen.**

God owes us nothing, we can pray to Him in hope, but this will not guarantee that He will do what we ask in precisely the way we ask Him to act.

Faith, obedience and trust in God's goodness will earn us eternal happiness with God, BUT we have no guarantee that what we pray for in our lives will happen. Faith in God gives us a measure of peace and tools that we can use in our live trials. This then gives us HOPE, HOPE THAT WE DESPERATELY NEED THROUGHOUT OUR LIVES, HOPE THAT WE WILL GAIN AND SHARE ETERNITY WITH OUR GOD.

When we are young however, (usually just grown up) with our hormones raging, our confidence soars, we believe that we are indestructible and that we know all that matters in our lives. We delight in choosing, what we want and strongly object to anyone who tries to advise and guide us as to how we should live our lives

. Our ideas and those of our generation are the only "**Cool ideas**", everything else is old fashioned, **belief in God is usually considered Un-Cool, boring, unimportant and old fashioned.**

How exciting it is to experiment with—Sex, Alcohol, Drugs, Gambling and so forth, we are strongly attracted to Trend setters, Glamour (people and things), power, danger, Sin, Evil, being daring, different, outrageous, in a word "Cool".

This is an incredibly dangerous time for us and can quite easily destroy the rest of our lives (both on earth and indeed our eternal life). This is the time that we need God most, but accept Him least. In our confidence and arrogance we fail to recognise any need for God and doubt His existence, luckily most of us manage to survive this period without permanent damage to our lives.

With the benefit of hindsight however, most of us then, gradually realise that at this age we should have listened more and accepted the guidance and direction given from those who loved us and wanted only the best for us and that—THEIR EFFORTS WERE FOR US, - BECAUSE THEY LOVED US if they didn't care about us they wouldn't have bothered to make the effort.

We truly need to accept that belief in God is "Cool" and that following God's will and living our lives accordingly really is the "Coolest thing" we can do, ---- indeed it is our only hope. If God does not exist then all the historical records, religious books, stories passed down to us, etc., are all lies, part of some huge conspiracy. Is this likely, ----- I think not.

As soon as we are ready to accept that there is a God it becomes necessary to establish what our relationship with Him should be. If we accept the fact that He was responsible for our creation and the creation of all that we perceive, then our very existence was caused by Him and can just as easily be terminated by Him, hence we should be in awe of what He can do to us. It therefore would be smart to know a little bit about Him, what He wants from us and how we can gain His favour.

As previously stated God is love incarnate He demands that we love Him above all and that we love our fellow man as ourselves. This command does NOT allow us to mistreat, harm, manipulate, exploit, enslave, suppress, pervert, ------etc. our fellow man.

God sent His son Jesus into our world to be a living example of how we should live our lives and abide by God's will with obedience and acceptance. **Jesus example is a marvellous guide to us as to how to find our way back to God**

My belief in God is the result of a lifetime of experience, reflective thought, observations, study and prayer. My beliefs did not come easily or casually. I have chosen to be a practising catholic as I believe this form of worship comes as close to what our God requires from us as any religion can. As previously stated I do not believe that being a practising catholic is the only path to God. –

It is however an excellent path to God.

Because we don't see God and have direct contact with Him, we cannot know with complete certainty that our beliefs regarding Him are correct in minute detail. This is why I am prepared to accept that He can and probably has manifested Himself in a number of religions whose teachings and practices are close enough to be acceptable to Him in what He wants from us. It therefore becomes sinful to condemn, ridicule and persecute followers of other religions for their concept of and service to God.

I believe that each of us is free to choose the path we follow. Prayer and reflection, openness to God's wishes, using our God given brain, will help us find our way. **The God we worship is the same one and only God. It does not matter weather you call Him Jesus, Jehovah, Allah,** or something else. He is the one and only God the creator of all that we perceive and He knows and listens to us when we pray to Him.

We should believe in and worship God because He truly is "ALL THAT THERE IS" He can and will satisfy all of our needs if we obey His will for us (HEAVEN). Without Him none of our needs will be met (HELL).

Chapter 9

WHAT AM I?

Trust and hope in God's guidance and help in your life.

What is the make up of a human being? **I believe we are BODY, MIND and SPIRIT.** The body and mind part of our make up is basically the same as all of God's living creation animals, birds, fish, etc. The spirit gives life to this combination but is very much more than what is given to the rest of living creation.

The spirit comes from God (His creation) but has a FREE WILL and CONCIOUSNESS which make it an independent entity. It controls the body and mind which are simply a direct result of the biological union of our parents.

The BODY provides the tools and means to react with our environment and a vehicle for our mind and spirit. It enables us to go and do what we imagine or think about. TO TAKE ACTION.

The MIND-(BRAIN) is like a super computer it can calculate and reason out problems and situations we encounter, it is rational and pragmatic in providing solutions. It records and stores all that happens to us, providing us with a data base on which we can draw when we encounter problems. Invariably it has far greater capacity than any other species of God's living creation.

The SPIRIT is far above the body and mind it gives life to them and uses them to fulfil your life's purposes, **whatever you choose these to be.** The body and mind are like a car and computer, the spirit is the car driver and computer operator. Consider the following scenario's ---

- A gang of louts attacks someone you love dearly (your mother, your little child). They are bigger, stronger, vicious and deadly, you have no possible chance of hurting them in any way. Your body feels very weak; your mind tells you it's hopeless to fight them. **But your spirit becomes enraged** and although completely terrified and without logical thought you attack them with all of your might.

- You have a retarded relative who looks strange and acts stupidly, you witness a group of youths taunting and making fun of your relative, and a couple of your close friends are in this group. Your mind tells you this is not important, keep your friends and don't antagonise the group. **Your spirit drives you to attack the group, defend your relative and break all contact with these (so called) friends.**

- You wish to be a great sportsman, your coach, your friends, your relatives, everyone you know tells you that you are hopeless, you will never amount to anything as a sportsman. **Your spirit tells you to strive mightily and ignore what these others think and you strive to do it any way.**

- A drowned man, doctors can remove the water in the man's lungs, connect a machine to cause his heart to beat, pump air into his lungs and pump blood through his body, but they can't restore his life, **his spirit has gone** the body and brain can still be intact (he has just died) but they to are dead without the spirit.

Your spirit never dies, it comes from God and will return to God and only God will judge it.

Your spirit is the very essence of you and can-------

- Fight on against hopeless odds.

- Love hopeless, useless, ugly, strange, different, weak and defenceless people.

- Persevere and strive on when everyone else has given up.

- Treasure and cling to life when all is lost.

HOWEVER, IT IS OF FUNDAMENTAL IMPORTANCE TO REALISE THAT ALL OF THE ABOVE ARE -- <u>POSITIVE ASPECTS OF THE SPIRIT,</u> YOU HOWEVER, ARE YOUR SPIRIT AND YOU HAVE FREE WILL. "<u>BEWARE</u>" THE NEGATIVE ASPECTS OF YOUR SPIRIT – <u>that could be a part of you.</u>

- At the prompting of the devil **you (your spirit)** can **also do untold evil**. Murderers, Rapists, Thieves, Paedophiles, Etc. embrace evil and become evil spirits. **You can welcome what the Devil tells you. ------"You can become the Devil's servant".**

- You can indulge yourself to extremes, celebrating your faults, giving in to your weaknesses (animal instincts we are born with). You can strive mightily for power, wealth, domination and exploitation of your fellow men and so forth. These are all wayward stirrings of your spirit, **which the Devil will delight in and use to manipulate you and ---- to claim your soul**

NOTE; the soul is another name for your spirit and is the essence of you. You may have happiness in this life, BUT YOU MAY LOSE YOUR SOUL FOR ETERNITY.

DON'T RISK YOUR SOUL EVER.

- **Your soul is you (your very essence) and will gain eternal happiness with God, or eternal torment when separated from God.** To fully answer the question, **WHAT AM I?** Involves a close, honest and deep introspection of yourself as an entity.

If you are just an intelligent animal then - **What is your purpose -indeed is there any?** Or is it only the goals that you set for yourself while you are alive, that you strive for, that give you purpose, OR perhaps an endless quest for pleasure and satisfaction.

WHAT YOUR PURPOSE IS------is virtually what defines your life.

THE FUNDAMENTAL PURPOSE OF OUR LIFE
IS TO OBEY GOD'S WILL FOR US SO THAT
WE CAN GAIN ETERNITY WITH GOD

<u>The devil will try everything he can to make you lose your soul; he will try to rubbish and twist the above thoughts and LIE, LIE, LIE--------------LIE to you about them.</u>

The Devil is very powerful, --- but God can and will help you to resist his lies, --- when you ask for help. NEVER LOSE GOD'S HELP! Ask God to guide and clarify your thoughts. Take the time and make the effort to establish what and where you are in all of this.

What about those who are handicapped, impaired, powerless, less than complete. What is their purpose and the significance of their life, - indeed is there any? God loves ALL OF US EQUALLY --- refer chapter 14 for a full discussion

WE ARE RESPONSIBLE FOR THE CHOICES WE MAKE— ALWAYS THINK ABOUT YOUR CHOICES ----AND THEIR CONSEQUENCES.

I believe we are our spirit, an independent entity, we choose a path to or away from God. Our journey towards God will provide peace and happiness – HEAVEN.

Our journey away from God will result in permanent separation from God, pain, loss, torment – HELL.

With our free will however, we choose our path and our choices are our responsibility.

NOTE! Our earthly lives are an insignificant blip of time, one second, WHEN COMPARED WITH ETERNITY. But in testing us--- <u>they establish our place in eternity</u>.

WHAT DOES MY LIFE MEAN, To me --- To those I love --- To those I know --- To all humanity – TO GOD? Think about this, you need to establish and work this out for yourself.

Refer to and reflect on the pictorial representation MY LIFE'S FLOW to help your thinking on this. Page 58

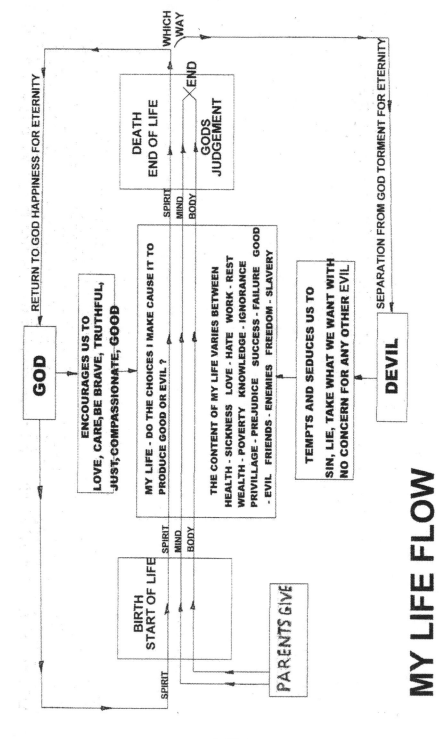

MY LIFE FLOW

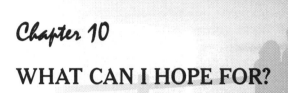

Chapter 10

WHAT CAN I HOPE FOR?

Trust and hope in God's guidance and help in your life.

Only God can satisfy all of our needs, God will always help those of us who try to help themselves, especially if we ask for His help. ------He does not however, do it for us and we do not know God's plans for the good of all of us. It never hurts our cause however, to pray to God for help, guidance and what we want in our life. .

Some peoples lives are filled with some or **all of the negatives listed below, they feel these intensely** and **these constitute a significant handicap in their lives.**

What is possible however is to transform these into the contrasting positives. What we need is faith and trust in God and the desire and motivation to change ourselves.

**ALL THINGS ARE POSSIBLE WITH
GOD'S HELP AND OUR EFFORT.**

How do you view your life and do you realise that.

NEGATIVES	Can change to	POSITIVES
My life is filled with	Can change to	God blesses me with
Anxiety, Panic, Mayhem	" " "	Peace, Calmness, Order
Helplessness	" " "	Resources and abilities
Fear and Dread	" " "	Courage and Hope
Emptiness	" " "	Fulfilment
Sadness	" " "	Joy
Lonesomeness	" " "	Love and Support
Confusion and uncertainty	" " "	Clarity, Purpose and Faith
Boredom, Tediousness	" " "	Joyous expectation
Uselessness, No self esteem	" " "	Competence and confidence
Weakness	" " "	Strength
Pain and Evil	" " "	Well Being and Goodness

Most of our feelings about ourselves are controlled and generated by our self image. Volumes have been written by various authors about this very important part of our make up and I do not intend to cover this here. I have recommended further reading on this subject at the end of this chapter.

Most importantly though religious books tell us that **we are created in God's image and likeness a little lower than the angels,** surely if this is true and I believe it is, we have nothing to be ashamed of and we can be proud of what our creator has given us and thank Him for this.

At this point let us consider some of the very unfortunate among us who are either impaired from birth, or due to disease or accident, some are in almost constant pain, some are so handicapped that they have no control over anything in their lives at all (they are completely dependent on others to keep them alive and for any of their day to day needs). A massive variety of degree's of impairment exist in our impaired. Those capable of creditable thought are frequently very bitter and ask the question, **"Why me, what have I done to deserve this?"**

There are no acceptable glib answers to this question. However, BELIEF IN GOD PROVIDES US WITH HOPE, God is our creator, He is all powerful, He loves us, He can and will help us either in this our earthly life (depending on His plans for the collective good of all of us)--- **or in our eternal life.**

Jesus the perfect son of God died in extreme pain out of love for us and set us the example of how to obey God's will with love and acceptance in spite of His own personal desires and fears. Jesus did not want to die, He was very frightened, terrified of what He knew He had to face, endure and pass through. He prayed that His Father would NOT REQUIRE Him to go through with it. Still He was prepared to endure all this horror if it was required, and it was. Jesus used his free will choosing to accept all that was required of Him.

His suffering served a purpose OUR SALVATION. Your suffering also serves a purpose, which is probably completely unknown to you, but requires your acceptance that it is part of God's plan for you and ALL OF US. If you accept this IN TRUST and believe that God knows what He is doing and in His goodness, you will draw strength from the following noting that.

- Intense pain is quickly forgotten once it is removed.

- All things pass, things that seem very important and never ending now, will fade into insignificance with sufficient time. **Eternity is absolutely long enough to make the memory of all pain and suffering fade into oblivion. Our earthly lives by comparison to our eternal lives, are insignificant blips in time.**

- Enduring (but ignoring) pain is a sound discipline used in training by great athletes, artists, performers, etc. to enable them to excel when they perform. This training blocks out the Devil's advantage of manipulating us when we sinfully indulge ourselves and conditions us for trials that we may have to face.

- Pain and trials, cause us to think and reflect and maybe this is necessary in our lives to ensure the salvation of our souls. This was the case in my life, I have been disciplined by God (Events in my life Chapter 13), by my parents and various people for (in retrospect) my greater good. When I review my life and look back on these trials, **which I rebelled against at the time, feeling outraged, deprived and abused.** With the benefit of hindsight I am glad and grateful that they occurred for **I believe they have helped and strengthened me on my path to God.**

WE MUST ALWAYS BEWARE THE DEADLY TRAP OF SELF PITY! We are very vulnerable and easily manipulated by the devil when we feel sorry for ourselves thoughts like "Poor me why did this have to happen to me" (a sure slippery slide into self pity). There is absolutely nothing wrong however with trying to improve your lot in life and we are free to do this by setting goals for ourselves. Goals are important and necessary in our lives.

WHY? Because ---

- They provide us with a target to aim for.
- A reason to act (motivation).
- They give us purpose and direction.

- They give us satisfaction and feed our ego and self esteem when we achieve them.

HOW IMPORTANT THESE GOALS ARE IN OUR LIVES HOWEVER, REQUIRES CAREFUL CONSIDERATION AND MONITORING. WE NEED TO THINK CLEARLY ABOUT WHAT GOALS WE SET FOR OURSELVES, AND IN WHAT PRIORITY.

NOTHING IS MORE IMPORTANT THAN THE GOAL OF SAVING OUR SOUL

ALL OF OUR LIVES OTHER GOALS SHOULD SUPPORT THIS – They become <u>Step Goals,</u> Sometimes we set **step goals** to achieve a **specific purpose, a major goal** and then lose sight of the MAJOR GOAL as we attempt to achieve the step goal. The step goal can become more important than the purpose for which it was set.

Be clear in your thinking, **ACHIEVE THE MAJOR GOAL OR PURPOSE.** Don't get bogged down or diverted in the step goals. Once again, our major goal should be

TO SAVE OUR SOUL, GAINING PEACE AND HAPPINESS WITH GOD FOR ETERNITY and ALL OTHER GOALS in our life SHOULD SUPPORT THIS.

How we feel about a particular goal being achieved is controlled by factors like.

- What this would mean financially.
- How our status would be effected.
- The effect on our colleagues, friends, family, competitors, Etc.
- What it means emotionally and spiritually.
- What it means to our business
- What this means in our life.

HOW HARD SHOULD WE STRIVE FOR OUR GOALS? This depends on their importance to us. How we feel about them. The factors influencing the goal, like timing, appropriateness, opportunity, achieve ability, etc.

We should not become fixated on a particular goal like in the song.-- "Once there was a silly old ram, Tried to knock a hole in a dam, No one could make that ram scram, He kept on butting that dam, He had high hopes, -------------------------" – All the ram could achieve is to bash his brains out This was an inappropriate goal for the ram. Similarly we should reconsider our goals from time to time. It may be necessary to abandon, revise, modify or replace a particular goal.

However, on matters effecting the spiritual well being of your spirit (soul), I believe that no compromise is possible.

THE SAVING OF YOUR SOUL MUST BE THE PRIMARY PURPOSE OF YOUR LIFE!

Consider martyrs—A MARTYR being one who chooses death in preference to doing something that will cost him to lose his spiritual soul. If happiness for all eternity with God is at stake,

<u>**WHAT WOULD YOU CHOOSE?**</u>
<u>**Pray that this ultimate sacrifice is not asked of you in your life.**</u>

Recommended Reading on self image psychology (referred to above)

PSYCHO-CYBERNETICS	Maxwell Maltz MD, F.I.C.S.
THE MAGIC POWER OF SELF IMAGE	" " " "
PSYCHOLOGY	

Chapter 11

HAPPINESS AN ATTITUDE OF GRATITUDE

Trust and hope in God's guidance and help in your life

When ever we compare ourselves to other people, we should always think about people who are worse off (not as blessed) as us. There will always be people both better off OR worse off than us.

> **Consciously choose to compare yourself with those who are worse off than you. Then thank God sincerely that you are not as badly off as them. BE GRATEFUL TO GOD FOR WHAT YOU HAVE BEEN GIVEN IN YOUR LIFE.**
>
> **DEVELOP AN ATTITUDE OF GRATITUDE for your lot in life.** *"I felt sorry for myself because I had no shoes. Then I met a man who had no feet."*

EXERCISE Close your eyes, now imagine that you are blind, you can't open your eyes, now put your fingers in both of your ears and imagine you are also deaf, you can't hear a thing, you are in a **black world of silence**. Now imagine trying to find your way home **(Blind and Deaf)** You would bump into people and all you would feel is them pushing and pulling at you, you can't see or hear anything, you can't communicate with them you are isolated and alone. **WHAT CAN YOU DO?**

THIS IS NIGHTMARE MATERIAL, THANK GOD FOR YOUR SIGHT AND HEARING remember that there are people with these afflictions. **How would you cope if you had these handicaps? Always think about what you have, NOT about what you don't have.**

THANK GOD FOR HIS GOODNESS AND DEVELOP AN--- <u>ATTITUDE OF GRATITUDE</u>, FOR ALL YOU ARE BLESSED WITH. There is nothing to stop you going after the things that you want. It is good to have goals and you can strive for the best in every thing. However, keep balance and moderation in all you do. **Practice and remember always to adopt an**

<u>**ATTITUDE OF GRATITUDE**</u>**, FOR ALL THAT YOU ARE BLESSED WITH.**

BE GRATEFUL FOR AND HAPPY WITH WHAT YOU HAVE IN YOUR LIFE.

EXERCISE. Make a list of all of your blessings. Pick out those things which mean the most to you and write them on a card which you carry with you. When you feel down, hurt, inadequate, etc., **Pull out your card, focus on and read it, fill your mind with your blessings and have them sustain you** through your down period. Put a lot of thought into your list, **<u>for it to work it must contain items that really mean something to you.</u> That you are grateful for and would feel very deprived without.** Following are some only items to start you thinking about what can you be grateful for?

- **People who really love you** Individuals, family, friends (animals-pets could be included).
- **Health and well being, the use of all your senses, limbs, brain, body.**

- **Opportunities you have,** social, education, work, sport, recreation, leisure, etc.

- **Freedom in the land you live in**, to be able to do and go where you want (without interference).

- **Talents (what you are good at) that you have** (invariably given to you by God at birth).

- **Wealth and opportunity, Job, Material possessions, Status, Etc.** (Australia is in the top 10% of countries in the world).

- **Safety, stability and social justice NOT** available in many many of the world's countries.

- **Stable, responsible and compassionate government in this country.**

THIS LIST IS NOT COMPLETE, TAKE THE TIME TO MAKE A LIST THAT REALLY MEANS SOMETHING TO YOU.

As previously stated. **Happiness is not earned it is given to us to accept and be happy.** We are like ungrateful children when we do not accept with gratitude what we have been given. **God is good, He doesn't need to be, but He is and He loves us and wants us to be happy. We owe it to ourselves and to God to be happy with what we have in this life.**

BE GRATEFUL FOR ALL OF THE BLESSINGS IN YOUR LIFE. DON'T ENVY, COVET OR LUST OVER WHAT OTHER PEOPLE HAVE. Just thank God for what you have!

You can however, strive to improve your happiness, together with the quality and content of your life (whatever you desire you are free to strive for).

Happiness however, comes from within ourselves and is based on our self image. If we believe we deserve happiness we can invariably find ways to be happy.

Happiness is independent of our actual state of existence but

rather on our beliefs or judgements regarding that state. Our feelings reflect what we think/judge our state to be (refer to the concept of Self Image Chapter 10 above)

Thoughts like the following <u>and the reasons you believe them</u>, effect your happiness.

To reflect reality a balance is necessary

NEGATIVE   POSITIVE

• I am a failure because--What I believe.   * I am successful in all that I do because--What I believe

• I am a Loser because – What I believe   * I am a Winner because – What I believe

• Every thing I try Fails, Look at "   * Every thing I try works because   "

• I am unloved because   "   * Everybody loves me because   ".

• I can't be happy because   "   * I'm always happy because   ".

• I am unlucky because   "   * Luck follows me in all that I do because "

All these thoughts reflect <u>our judgement </u>of our self and lead to SELF PITY OR FEELINGS OF SUPERIORITY

THEY SHOULD REFLECT A BALANCED REALITY You can change your perspective and the way you think about these things. Remember that **you are created in God's image and likeness by a God who loves you so greatly, that He sent His only son to be tortured and killed in the most horrible manner, to save you, and that He has given you so much (list you have made above). He wants you to be happy.**

IT IS THEREFORE ALL BUT A DUTY & OBLIGATION FOR US TO BE HAPPY, to be grateful to God for all that He has given us. There are virtually unlimited reasons for us to be happy. We however, have to search out, ACCEPT and acknowledge these in our minds. Review Chapter.10 "What can I hope for" this will help you form your attitude as POSITIVE and PURPOSEFUL to achieve HOPE AND HAPPINESS.

Some of the happiest people that I have met in my life have been

the very poorest and most deprived in terms of material possessions. They were just happy and content with their lives PERIOD. This is a wholesome, healthy and worthwhile attitude to adopt and one that will help us throughout our lives.

THE ATTITUDE TO YOUR LIFE THAT YOU CHOOSE TO ADOPT IS ONE OF THE MOST CRUCIAL CHOICES THAT YOU WILL MAKE IN YOUR LIFE AND WILL EFFECT EVERY AREA OF YOUR LIFE

Chapter 12

PRAYER

Trust and hope in God's guidance and help in your life.

When we pray we talk to God, the creator of the universe, of us and of all that we perceive. The fact that He loves us and wants a relationship with us is a huge privilege and blessing for us. He does not need us, we are His creation to do with as He pleases. **It is overwhelming that in our insignificance He loves us.** A similar situation would be for us to treasure and love an ant, slug, worm or similar.

It follows therefore that a litany of "I want this and that" type communications show a complete lack of reverence and respect for God. God is there for us and He knows our needs and desires, He loves us and will grant our prayers if they are good for us and fit in with His plans for the collective good of all of us. Like a child asking their parent for a shiny cut throat razor or a loaded pistol **He will not grant requests which will hurt or harm us.**

Still like a loving parent He will always try to help us with what we desire and strive for.

Never however forget who it is that you are talking to when you pray and always be grateful to God for all the blessings that He has poured into your life. MAKE SURE THAT YOU THANK GOD SINCERELY FOR ANY PRAYER YOU HAVE MADE THAT HE RESPONDS TO.

A good example of how to pray is given to us in the bible with Jesus talking to his father---**The Lord's Prayer or "Our Father".**

> **Our Father who art in heaven,**
> **Hallowed be thy name,**
> **Thy kingdom come,**
> **Thy will be done on earth as it is in heaven,**
> **Give us this day our daily bread,**
> **And forgive us our trespassers as we forgive those who**
> **trespass against us.**
> **And lead us not into temptation,**
> **But deliver us from evil,**
> **For Thine is the kingdom, the power and the glory**
> **forever and ever,**
> **Amen.**

Whenever we talk to God this is a fine example of how to.

A simple technique or method to organise your thinking and direct your prayer in a thought out practised ritual is to use the words Faith and Altar in the following manner. **Note spell Faith as (F- A-L-T-H) use the letters to guide your thoughts in your prayer**

Letter	Thought	Sample Prayer
F	Faith	Dear Lord I believe and trust in you
A	Adore	Dear Lord I adore you from your hands I came and with you I will be happy Forever
L	Love	Dear Lord I love you, I love you, I love you, please help me to love you daily more and more.
T	Thank	Dear Lord Thank you for all that you have done for me and for the countless gifts and blessings that you pour into my life.
H	Hope	Dear Lord please help me — What you ask for in your prayers.

Similarly you can use the word ALTAR

A	Adore	Similar to above		
L	Love	"	"	"
T	Thank	"	"	"
A	Ask	"	"	"
R	Resolve	Dear Lord I promise to do better in my life by –		

Your own heartfelt thoughts poured out to God when you are emotionally ravaged and upset can be better than any mechanical learned prayers or rituals, remember though that Faith, Respect, Hope, Trust and Love are the key elements.

- **Faith in our God is an essential ingredient in any prayer to God. Why would our God respond to any prayer made to Him if there is no faith, hope or trust in Him by the person who makes the prayer.** These type of prayers become mechanical recitals, verbal utterances, babble (almost an insult to God) ---- **<u>Faith, Trust and Hope in God, are the keys to successful prayer.</u>**

- Once again God is an infinite source of all that we could possibly need or desire and He will grant our requests if they are good for us, on our spiritual journey to Him and they do not detract from His plans for the collective good of all of us.

- **He wants to help us because He loves us and we are vitally important to Him, as our history and religious books reveal.** Hence our prayers to Him in faith, hope and trust have a huge chance of success. ---**Prayers are powerful when we have faith— when we actually believe God can and will help us.**

- **His help may not come to us in the exact way we expect, but it will come to us when we have faith.**

Why He would want to help us is ---- BECAUSE HE LOVES US MORE THAN WE COULD EVER KNOW and HE CONSIDERS US THE MOST SIGNIFICANT PART OF HIS CREATION.

Faith, Hope and Trust in God and Belief in His teachings (bible etc.). Provides me with a framework, a reference guide, or yardstick to help me to evaluate and assign importance to issues I face in my life

- This then gives me confidence and perspective in these issues and helps me find peace when I am in turmoil.
- Gives me courage when I am frightened.
- Gives me clarity and confidence when I am confused and don't know what to do.
- Gives me hope when I am hopeless, and in a state of despair.
- Provides me with a feeling of well being and confidence that Justice will prevail and that the glaring inequities in our world will be righted either now, or in our eternal life with God --- **for eternity.**

I pray to God to strengthen my faith. I reread and review the books that I have written to replenish, reaffirm my thinking and further strengthen my faith, using these books as tools for this purpose throughout my life. Life is not over until it's over and the Devil is very patient and persistent using all his powers to tempt and pervert us away from God and the truth of our reality.

Our struggle will continue throughout our lives, **we have not won -- until we are one with God. Be warned our fight is ongoing, don't drop your guard or rest on your laurels. The Devil will strike when you least expect it and when he believes you are most vulnerable, times when your faith is weak at a low, when you doubt.**

God is our only hope and protection; never hesitate to call on His help when you are in danger. Remember God loves us more than we

will ever know He wants our success and will help us all He can, He is our friend and protector, accept this fact with trust and faith.

<u>None of us impose on, or upset our God by praying to Him for help.</u>

WE CAN TRUST IN HIM, WE CAN HOPE IN HIM.

His help and Love for each and every one of us is a <u>resource that is limitless</u>. So use this resource to help you through ALL of your life trials. Pray to God with confidence, HAVE FAITH THAT HE WILL HELP YOU, TRUST IN GOD AND NEVER FORGET TO THANK HIM WHEN HE RESPONDS TO YOUR PRAYERS.

Prayers are incredibly powerful because they are heard by God, this has been proved time and again in our history. Prayers keep God in our lives, and in our consciousness and that is a healthy and wholesome trait to develop in our lives.

PRAYER IS COMMUNICATION WITH THE VERY SOURCE OF ALL THAT WE PERCEIVE IN OUR REALITY AND GIVES US THE HOPE THAT OUR PRAYERS WILL BE GRANTED

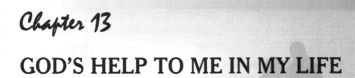

Chapter 13

GOD'S HELP TO ME IN MY LIFE

Trust and hope in God's guidance and help in your life.

God has helped me throughout my life when I needed Him most. **I will focus on His help with "Julie", my profoundly handicapped daughter** and mention only that His help has been a constant in my life and significantly in. The help He gave my family and I in our brutal internment of three and a half years in a Japanese prisoner of war camp, in the 2nd World War, how we all survived and our repatriation in Australia after the war. And His help to my wife and I in the raising of our six children (including Julie).

"JULIE"- A Miracle of life

When my daughter Julie was born, I was twenty four years old and already the father of two children who were aged two and one. In 1965 it was not the practice for fathers to be present at their child's birth, and as my wife had had very long deliveries with our other two children. I dropped my wife at the hospital and joined our first born, while we awaited the new birth.

Within four hours I was summoned urgently to the hospital and met by the attending doctor who told me gravely that my child had been born, but that she was **profoundly handicapped and would not survive the night.** In an emotional fog I am ashamed to confess that I was secretly relieved to have the burden of raising another child apparently removed.

Against these odds however, Julie survived the night. She was then transferred to a specialist children's hospital the following morning. Here one of the countries leading paediatricians informed me that it would be impossible for Julie to survive more than a few days as something had gone very wrong in my wife's early pregnancy and Julie was profoundly retarded and more than that she had suffered severe brain damage during childbirth. This caused Julie to be Blind, Deaf, Spastic and Autistic (even though she had perfectly good beautiful blue eyes).

Despite all these odds however Julie continued to survive, her life hanging by a thread as it moved from crises to crisis. Four months later things stabilised and I was now advised by Julie's doctors that it would be impossible for Julie to survive more than a year.

Forty four years later, Julie still clung to life (she died 4 weeks after her 44th. birthday). Over the years I have wondered at the purpose of Julie's life. Strangely enough she was no burden to bear as at every crises in her life, torturous health conditions, financial hardships, difficulty in child raising, huge emotional stress and so forth. God provided us with a positive outlook and solutions to all the problems we encountered.

It only struck me recently that the odds of Julie's survival were like asking an unarmed, defenceless man to walk a hundred meters across an open field racked by machine gun fire. With normal unimpaired people a feat of this nature, **that is survival against impossible odds, usually generates great acclaim.** Remember Stewart Driver's survival in the landslide at Thredbo alpine village. He survived after being trapped and desperate for all of two days. His ordeal generated huge, massive acclaim and applause when he was rescued.

Julie's chances were far less than his, she survived her forty four

years trapped and desperate in her world and yet her story is unknown and her endurance and heroism is unrecognised. Her survival is all the more remarkable and heroic when you realise that because of her disabilities. **Julie was completely isolated in a silent, black world unable to draw any emotional support, encouragement, love or help from any other human being, isolated by her Autism.**

The pains, anxieties and trials she endured, she faced alone, **"ALONE, COMPLETELY ISOLATED,-- EXCEPT FOR GOD'S HELP -- like she was the only person on this planet, without any control over anything in her life, her life literally just happening to her.**

<u>**All Julie could do throughout her whole life was to ENDURE EVERYTHING that came up - without any control of anything in her life and – To hang on as best she could!**</u>

Julie was indeed a living, breathing Miracle of Life. Her continued survival illustrated that only God decides when we die and demonstrates that hope is possible even when faced with impossible odds. We can therefore take heart and learn from Julie that **with God's love we can endure and continue even with no apparent hope.**

Whenever I am tempted to feel sorry for myself, I think of Julie and what she had to endure and thank God for the content of my life. God helped me throughout Julie's life with every problem encountered. **I search for meaning in all of this and realise how little I know.**

JULIE IS MY HERO as I realise with awe and admiration that Julie made the most of the content of her life without giving up, she simply got on with it.

<u>A CHAMPION PERFORMANCE</u>

I wish that I could share some profound insight with you as to life's meaning and purpose and perhaps one is, **that all we can do (like Julie) is to hang on and appreciate what we have in our lives, using**

what we have been given to do the best we can. ----In the game of life we have to play the cards we have been dealt----- and make the most of what we have.

I hoped and prayed that Julie had some happiness in her life and I think she did for she smiled, clapped her hands and appeared content and happy at times in spite of what she had to constantly endure. I thanked God for these periods.

I trust that God will now make Julie perfect and reward her with the happiness that Julie's life of pain, deprivation and suffering has surely earned for her. I trust that all the memories Julie has of her earthly life will now fade into oblivion as she shares eternity with the loving God who created her.

Without God, Julie's life and all it contained, would have had no purpose or meaning what so ever. With God, Julie's life with all its pain and hardship did have a meaning, causing all who encountered Julie to marvel at her endurance, ponder and think about their own lives and reflect on life in general – her life had "HOPE" for her and for all of us.

GOD'S HELP TO ME WAS IN THE PRACTICALITIES REQUIRED IN COPING WITH ALL THE NEEDS ASSOCIATED WITH JULIE'S LIFE, THEIR EFFECT ON MY WIFE, MY FAMILY AND ME. THE INSIGHTS AND REALITY PERCEPTIONS HER LIFE PROVIDED TO ALL OF US AND THE HEALING PEACE AND GRACE GOD GAVE US THAT ENABLED US TO COPE

I believe that Julie's life while horrible for her was a perfect example to all of us as to how we should live our lives. By making the most of what she had been given and simply getting on with her life she showed us how we should live our lives. We can and should bear in mind that our earthly lives are but a short blip in eternity and that hopefully we can look forward to our eternal lives for joy and an end to all our suffering

Chapter 14

HOW DO WE RECONCILE INTELLIGENCE OR LACK THEREOF WITH OUR SPIRITUAL LIFE

Trust and hope in God's guidance and help in your life.

How do we reconcile intelligence and lack thereof with our spiritual life? My daughter Julie was born into this world with **overwhelming handicaps**, she was deaf, blind, spastic and autistic she had no usable intelligence and virtually nothing that she could use or identify as beneficial in her life.

The cards, she was dealt in "the game of life", were the worst possible hand imaginable. She lived in a black world of silence, her handicaps would make it seem as though she was alone, alone completely isolated, virtually the only person on this planet.

She faced everything that constituted her life ALONE. She could not recognise or respond to love, help or support from any other person (her autism). She faced her life and existed in it <u>alone, alone, alone</u>, she could only endure everything that happened to her--- constant darkness, not a sound, operations, huge periods of pain, sickness, constant deprivation, nothing explained and nil control over anything in her life. She was forced into all her life activities without any preamble, explanation, reassurance or comfort.

A small example of this nightmare, that I witnessed directly, occurred while Julie was in hospital, she required intravenous feeding and a tube for this purpose had to be shoved up her nose and down her throat into her stomach. She's blind and deaf and completely uncomprehending. She was held by one nurse while another stared inserting the tube, this hurt her and she tried to grab the offending tube to stop the hurt, this only resulted in the nurse holding her more forcibly to prevent her trying to defend herself. She started to cry, can you imagine what you would feel in her place, unknown people forcibly holding you and inflicting pain on you in a black world of silence

"AN ABSOLUTE NIGHTMARE"

This was Julie's life and so it went on and on --- literately just happening to her all she could do was to endure everything and accept it, or die. The necessities of life food, warmth, shelter etc. were all that could be provided for her, communication, explanation, emotional support encouragement, love that she could feel and comprehend were impossible.

The only possible emotional and spiritual help she could get would have come from God. I believe, God did help her, as there were periods in her life when she laughed, clapped her hands and seemed happy. She was a perfect example of how to accept life as it is, regardless of its content, try to make the best of it and get on with it—against all the odds and hardships, Julie lived for forty four years

Julie's ability to think and intelligence were completely unknown to any of us and appeared completely non existent, from our point of view. Yet her ability to overcome all the medical hardships, pain, sickness, deprivations and accidents in her life was nothing short of miraculous. She heroically endured ALL, accepted ALL, and got on with her life. Her spirit overcame the massive deficiencies of mind and body in her life and she carried on living her life regardless of its content.

When she was born and during her early life I could not see any purpose or point in her continued survival and this severely tested my faith and belief in God's goodness.

Over the years of her life however, I witnessed her courage, fortitude, endurance and acceptance of what constituted her life and gradually, with awe and admiration, it dawned on me how heroic, marvellous and tenacious her struggle to survive was. I now believe Julie's life was an example to all of us, who were a part of her life, for she showed us how to accept life as it is, make the most of what you have and get on with it.

Belief in God's promises and goodness now make me happy for Julie as I realise her earthly trials and pains are finally over. I believe she is now perfect, unimpaired in any way and enjoys happiness with our God for eternity. All her earthly trials, pains, etc. which she endured for forty four years will now fade into oblivion as eternity proceeds.

Julie's life reinforces my belief that our composition is Body, Mind and Spirit and that our spirit does not die it returns to God and will be judged by Him.

Our spirit or soul is the essence of us. On our journey through our lives our choices and obedience to God's will, in the trials that we face determine our spiritual place in eternity, when God judges us.

How then do we reconcile intelligence and/or lack thereof with our spiritual life? The above shows us that disabled and handicapped people may well be much closer to and more acceptable to our God than thinking intelligent people give them credit for.

Intelligence, prompts us to think that we are superior to those of us who have much less of it, -- or none of this gift from God. This is not necessarily so as our thinking ability causes us to question everything and requires us to make sense of all that we perceive. We can easily become judgemental and superior in our attitude to life and to others, who we now consider less capable than we are.

Furthermore, we may even dismiss and discount their worth and not recognise their spiritual significance to the God who created them without these gifts and blessings, gifts which most of us just take for granted

The disabled are spiritual entities equivalent to any of us (who are blessed with intelligence etc.) Their minds and bodies may well be hugely impaired BUT, they are equally -precious to God as any of us--- even though we are more blessed with superior abilities and intelligence (GIFTS that we haven't earned, but that we received from God at birth).

GOD WILL JUDGE EACH OF US INDIVIDUALLY FOR OUR CHOICES AND THE USE OF WHAT WE AS INDIVIDUALS --- HAVE BEEN GIVEN

Think and reflect on this at length, there is a mountain of revelation in these issues and they will greatly influence us in our attitude to life.

WHAT ATTITUDE TO LIFE DO YOU ADOPT? As stated exhaustively, it is hugely beneficial to adopt an "ATTITUDE OF GRATITUDE" for all that you are blessed with.

You will choose either consciously or unconsciously your attitude to life and this choice is yours to make, your responsibility. Don't blame anyone else for the choices you make.

In making your choice think about people like Julie who struggle daily to survive. They endure all the pains, hardships, lack of control, anxieties, and fears their lives contain --- but they still cling to each and every blessing in their life and get on with it as best as they can.

Be very grateful that you don't have a huge burden of this nature or similar to carry. Make the most of what you have in your life and simply get on with it.

Chapter 15

RELIGIOUS BOOKS OUR HISTORY

Trust and hope in God's guidance and help in your life.

Historical books are largely accepted as a record of what occurred before we were born, usually they are written by the winners of wars, that is the people in power during a particular period of our past. The authors may have some bias in their presentation of what occurred and historians often debate at length some of the details. However, hopefully they provide at least a reasonable account of what actually happened.

Similarly, religious books are graphic accounts written by witnesses to the events they describe, when these concur with the historical books written, there is a fair chance that they are accurate in the information they provide. The bible accounts of the life of Jesus Christ and historical accounts of the events that occurred 2000 years ago do not conflict significantly, hence there is a good possibility that they are accurate in what they report to us.

A lot of what is written in some cultures and with most indigenous people are I believe cultural fables used by one generation of people to pass on moral values and concepts of imagined Gods to their offspring giving them a plan and guide for living (Greek and Roman Mythology, Aboriginal dreaming, Fairy-tales and so forth). These are usually symbolic imaginations and in no way represent factual accounts of past happenings or events (all pure fiction).

When God designed us, I believe He gave us an instinct to find Him (our God) to provide purpose and meaning to our lives. His creation gives us glimpses of His power and love of us. Our attempts to find God and respond to Him over our history has resulted in a massive collage of Gods for every occasion, gods of war, beauty, fertility, wine, peace., light, Sun, Moon, -----and so on.

I believe that God exists as explained in chapters 1 and 2 of this book. The evidence of His existence surrounds us. His immense power and infinite capacity are beyond comprehension. I am in awe of what He must be AND AM CONCIOUS OF MY INSIGNIFICANCE COMPARED TO HIM.

HOW HE WOULD KNOW ME, LET ALONE LOVE ME IS UNKNOWN TO ME however, the evidence of His love for each of us is proclaimed in nearly all significant religious books. These books are supported by historical records in a lot of what they proclaim.

I choose to believe that these are largely true. I am sceptical about the written account of the worlds creation, Adam and Eve and the concept that Heaven is up there (where?) and hell down below (again where?).

We now know about our planet, it's position in our solar system and our solar system's position in the universe and because we have uncovered these truths we could in our arrogance proclaim that Bible accounts of ascensions into Heaven (up there) and damnation into Hell (below) are untrue.

However, quantum mechanics revels the possibility of parallel universes and many concepts far beyond the current state of comprehension of most of us. I believe that God in His wisdom is slowly revealing more and more of His mind to us, **entry into a parallel universe could explain these bible accounts,**-- as described in books on the subject, parallel universes exist in the same place and at the same time but are entirely separate to each other and inaccessible to each other. **God however could enable access**

It is possible that when Jesus ascended into Heaven (Bible acct. Luke 24, 50-53) He went into a parallel universe (Heaven) rather than a waiting space ship or other obscure possibility. The bible accounts are possible when considered along these lines. We are so insignificant compared to our God but with a huge capacity for arrogance and pride in our achievements and doubts concerning anything we don't fully understand, this frequently causes us to doubt God's existence and holy book readings.

HERE AGAIN IS THE ON GOING DANGER, THAT WE LIKE LUCIFER THINK THAT WE DO NOT NEED THE GOD THAT CREATED US, OR THAT GOD DOES NOT EXIST

THAT WE IN FACT, KNOW IT ALL. Our egos are large and our knowledge is small, but still we think we know it all. God has I believe appeared to some of us and inspired and empowered these people to lead large numbers of us to Him (our God) these are the founders, saints and prophets of various religions.

I believe that there is only one God and that in essence there is very little difference in his instructions to us in

- **All Christian religions**
- **Islamic religions**
- **Jewish religions**

The message in essence of all these books (Bible, Koran, Torah) is the same, love of God, our fellow man and good works, it is only man's interpretation and manipulation of these messages that causes individuals to promote hatred, bias and evil endeavours. Proclaiming that this passage means this or that and acting accordingly

The fact that there is so much turmoil in the ranks of all these religions, with one group claiming superiority over another generating conflict and hatred between groups, merely points out the effectiveness of the Devil's lies to us and our own built in pride and arrogance. If we get back to God's basic instructions we will not go wrong. Once again

WE MUST LOVE THE LORD OUR GOD WITH OUR WHOLE HEART AND SOUL, WITH ALL OUR STRENGTH AND WITH ALL OUR MIND.----and WE MUST LOVE OUR NEIGHBOUR AS OURSELVES.

Lawyers and manipulators have great joy in arguing what passages of the bible and other religious books mean and easily distort what was intended in the writing. Don't be deceived, ask God's help and use the brain God has given you to guide your life.

ALWAYS STICK TO GOD'S ABOVE COMMANDS. Remember the miseries, persecutions, oppressions and wars caused by people proclaiming they are doing it for God. What an obscenity! ---- It becomes clear who is really behind these triumphs of evil!

THE DEVIL, INTENSELY EVIL AS ALWAYS.

Some of the passages in the old testament of the bible seem to contradict what Jesus teaches us in the new testament about our loving God. For example 2 Kings 9, 1 to 37 and 10, 1 to 31. Here apparently God orders the death of all of the followers of Baal (men, women and children) the brutality involved in these and other passages of the old testament contradicts and confuses what I believe God wants from us. I place my trust in God but if these passages are recorded correctly then my comprehension of God's wishes for us is less than complete.

There is absolutely no way that I would oppose or claim any moral superiority to the God who created me. My ability to think and reason is a gift from God (which I treasure) but I accept His authority and will in everything (specially what I don't understand), I am however

sceptical about and doubt the accuracy and detail of some of these passages (I don't automatically accept that this is the inspired word of God and that these actions represent God's will). I pray to God to guide my life's choices, I trust in His guidance and use my intellect to determine what action if any--- He requires from me.

This is where each of us must make our own moral decisions as to what we believe Our God wants from us. Further,----- it does NOT give us the right to condemn and ridicule other people for their heart felt beliefs in God.

I believe The teachings of Jesus in the new testament are correct and reflect much more accurately the image of our God. **This is why I caution against blindly accepting that all of what is written is the word of God.** I believe that God is consistent in what He wants from us and the murder and mayhem in some of these passages **do not** reflect God's will for us

Our lives are all about making choices and we are responsible for the choices we make so choose carefully. **PRAY TO GOD AND ASK HIS HELP FOR YOU TO CHOOSE WELL.**

Religious books have in most cases been written by sincere people sharing their beliefs and recording what they have been witness to, we can invariably profit from their accounts however, always test what has been written with God's instructions to us and reason out what is written in the light of your own experience. **Never accept what is written on someone else's say so or because IT IS WRITTEN. If the subject matter is important, but a confusing shades of grey issue, ask God's help to clarify the matter for you. Some sincere people believe the bible and other books are the inspired word of God, which can not be contradicted and live their lives accordingly,** you will need to decide for yourself what constitutes God's will in your life.

**IT IS VERY IMPORTANT TO WORK
THIS OUT FOR YOURSELF.**

We should use religious books as an aid and guide to living our lives as God would want. Do not however follow obscure passages and others interpretations to do anything that conflicts with God's basic instructions.

LOVE OF GOD, TRUST IN HIM AND FOLLOWING HIS WILL FOR US, WILL RETURN US TO HIM.------RELIGIOUS BOOKS CAN HELP US GREATLY IN OUR LIFE'S SEARCH FOR GOD. THEY MUST NOT DOMINATE OUR THINKING HOWEVER AND CAUSE US TO DO ANYTHING OPPOSITE TO LOVING GOD AND OUR FELLOW MAN.

Chapter 16

WHAT DOES GOD THINK OF US/ME?

Trust and hope in God's guidance and help in your life.

It would be exceedingly presumptuous of me to claim that I know what God thinks of us, however, what follows is a reasoned approach to some of the evidence we have available.

- **He loves us with unconditional love.** This is hard to understand when we reflect on what we collectively have done over the ages—Oppression, Slavery, Persecution, Perversion, Sadism, Murder, Etc. as Countries, Sects, Groups and individuals. **STILL GOD'S LOVE IS THERE FOR US.**- Examples from the Bible are The Prodigal Son (Luke 15 11-31), The good Samaritan (Luke 10 20-36)

- He would be disappointed with a lot of our actions but like the ever hopeful parent, He thinks that we can and will change. He sent His son to live and die amongst us to show us how to live our lives with love, obedience and acceptance (His example is our guide)

- He is capable of anger when our behaviour degenerates to complete perversion or revolt against His will (examples From the bible)

- The Deluge --- (Genesis 7 1-24)

- The Destruction of Sodom and Gomorrah --- (Genesis 19 1-29)

- The Egyptian Plagues and drowning in Red Sea— (Exodus 1-15)

If I were in God's place viewing the actions of the people that I had created and their indifference and disobedience, I would probably wipe them out and start again. The fact that God hasn't done this demonstrates **His ongoing love for us and His trust in our choices,**

THIS IS OUR ONLY HOPE!

Our future is in our own hands, and once again it is not all Doom and Gloom as there are quite a number of us who try to live their lives according to God's plan and instructions to us. There is goodness, Love, self sacrifice, courage, good works and many other virtues practised by many of us. **Some of us devote our whole lives in providing care, help and love to the most deprived amongst us. My hope is that more and more of us will join the ranks of these good people to provide heaven for all of us.** Once again we have free will, we have been shown the way, what will we choose?

What God thinks of us will become apparent when we die and God judges us, hopefully, we will not be found wanting and hopefully God's love for us and our love for God will triumph generating happiness with God for all eternity **(HEAVEN)** .

"What does God think of us "we can personalise it by thinking "What does God think of me" (or rather you, the reader of this book). What is intended, is for each of us to reflect upon our individual relationship with the God, who created us. Imagine yourself as an independent observer of you in your life, try to establish how you feel about the person you are observing. Assess this persons deeds, his relationship with all those he associates with and his treatment of them. Assess his goals, dreams and aspirations, how do you judge this person?

What do you think would help this person? Again how do you feel about this person? - **And this person is you**

God is love incarnate. With all His power, superiority and majesty as our creator, **why should GOD love us? This is truly a mystery,** as we have so many faults. His commands to us are, **to love Him and our fellow man,** this is true for all major religions. We however, disobey, distort and ignore His commands. We produce sinners, terrorists, suicide bombers, ---- we murder, oppress and have contempt for others, this can't be a way to God and yet it happens all the time. ---- Where does this come from? **THINK ABOUT THIS! In my mind these acts come direct from the Devil using us as his tools.** We are more vulnerable to the Devil's lies and manipulation when we are stressed, dissatisfied, angry, rebellious, feeling sorry for ourselves, envious of others, afraid and so forth.

The Devil's lies are much more convincing at these times and we find release to our stress in believing him. Are we so gullible? --- Apparently we are. ---- When you think about it, how can we be so stupid?

The danger is that we will lose our souls, THE ULTIMATE CALAMITY. We need to be very wary and on our guard against the Devil's manipulations. But are we? THINK ABOUT YOUR OWN LIFE AND BEHAVIOUR! -------ARE YOU IN DANGER NOW?

We are incomplete without God. **All our searching, frenzied activity, plans, hopes and dreams will do nothing for us----- unless, they lead us to God.**

God is the source of peace, joy, satisfaction and love that we so desperately need, HEAVEN is our permanent return to the God who created us. Forced separation from God, means that none of our needs are met (HELL). Are you prepared to risk your soul to gain earthly victory in your "short" earthly life but sacrifice your soul --- for all eternity?

Imagine if you were God, how would you feel about you as a

person? Now mentally assess what this person could do to improve his relationship with God. You are this person, set your goals from your heart and go for it.

In the 1st person think about God and me, talk and pray to God, your friend. Bring God into every part of your life. Your relationship will develop consistent with your heartfelt innermost feelings and desires. Think, reflect, and deliberate

GOD AND ME, THAT'S ALL THAT MATTERS.

ETERNITY, HOW LONG IS THAT?

Trust and hope in God's guidance and help in your life.

Time is a strange concept, as children we sometimes seem to wait forever for some event or milestone to occur in our lives. Then as we get older time seems to fly and we find it hard to understand where the time has gone. We reach "Old Age" and find it very hard to account for our time here.

We read history books which tell us about people and events that occurred a long time before we were born, I try to gain a tangible perspective on these events by considering approximately how many lifetimes (birth to death) these times represent.

If we take the average lifetime over the preceding centuries as fifty years (a reasoned average) **then----**

2 000 years = 40 lifetimes, **40 people were born lived their whole life & died, one after another**

5 000 years = 100   "   **100** " " " " " " " " " " " " "

1 000 000 " = 20 000   "   **20 000** " " " " " " " " " " " " "

All these lifetimes, as one ends another starts. We have excellent depiction's in movie s and books of what it would have been like to be alive in those times .Our imaginations can generate the emotions and feelings of what it would have been like for us .The actual newsreels and photographs of people and events are direct window's into the past,**we see the images (actual photographs and movies) and we can be there in our imagination.**

Happenings in our own lives however, we know and experience directly and are therefore the most important to us because we are directly involved, **we know and feel all the emotions, victories and losses associated with these events, ------THIS INDEED. IS OUR LIFE.**

The events that occur to us and around us in the rest of the world may be All Consuming, Earth Shattering and Immense, we may be in continuous pain (physical or mental) and it may seem never ending (our whole life after all) --- **YET ALL THINGS PASS EXCEPT ETERNITY.**

How important is our earthly life then, compared to eternity and how does our life compare with all those lives ------ who have gone before us ------ or are yet to come?

LUCKILY, WE DON'T HAVE TO WORRY ABOUT THIS, all we need to answer for is our own lives and this remains and always is OUR RESPONSIBILITY.

If we believe in God and that we are not just intelligent animals, that we truly do have a soul, then Eternity is of huge importance to us, FOR WE WILL BE THERE AS IT UNFOLDS.

OUR PLACE IN IT, WILL BE DETERMINED BY OUR GOD WHEN HE JUDGES US FOR THE CHOICES WE HAVE MADE IN OUR LIVES. Most of us will not reach one hundred years of age, **so how important is our lives and all they contain, if they do not win us the PRIZE OF HEAVEN AND HAPPINESS FOR ETERNITY.**

Let us consider some concepts of eternity---------how long is it?

- If a little bird flew down from the sky and brushed it's wing against the earth only once a year. How many years would it take to wear the world away? --------- **AN ETERNITY**

- For those interested in mathematics 1 000 000 000 raised to the power of 1 000 000 000 1 billion multiplied by itself 1 billion times in years. ------------- **AN ETERNITY**

- One grain of sand compared with the total number of grains of sand on every beach, sand hill desert, etc. of every country in our world as a number of years. --- **AN ETERNITY**

The numbers involved are overwhelming and yet with all these concepts, at the end of these times you could then say -----" **well that's only the beginning.** "

How paltry then does the length of our earthly lives seem by comparison and how wonderful it would be to be at peace and happy for all of Eternity

THIS IS WHAT IS PROMISED TO US BY GOD IF WE OBEY HIS WILL FOR US.

Scientists have calculated the timing of the start of our universe **the big bang approx. 14 billion years ago** and also the end of life as we know it on our planet which will apparently occur when our sun becomes a red giant, as its nuclear fuel runs out causing it to collapse in a super nova explosion something like **500 million years from now.** What then is, the significance of our lives in all of this? If our spirits are indeed still around, have the choices we made during our lives earned us Peace and Happiness with the God who created all of this and with whom we now share Eternity

WHAT DO YOU THINK?

Chapter 18

ANOTHER PERSPECTIVE OF EVIL

Trust and hope in God's guidance and help in your life.

The Devil (Satan) and his followers, all devils in hell, want our downfall, they want us to fail in our attempts to gain Heaven by following God's will during our earthly life trials. They will do all in their power to cause us to fail.

<u>Devils are subtle and clever liars who enter our thinking to twist our reality so that we -</u>

- Give in to weaknesses that we have and indulge in our sinful desires.
- Get confused, arrogant, bored, doubting God's existence.
- Hurt others, and treat them unjustly.
- Do wrong, **indulge in sin and evil.**
- Blame God, other persons, events and so forth for our earthly misfortunes.
- Give the devil power by believing his lies, committing sins and **much worse becoming his willing servant.**

WITH OUR FREE WILL WE, MAKE OUR CHOICES AND WE HAVE TO LIVE

WITH THE CONSEQUENCES OF THOSE CHOICES. --------- FOR ETERNITY.

HISTORICAL REFLECTION REVEALS THAT MOST CATASTROPHES IN LIFE, ARE MAN MADE, THROUGH INDIVIDUAL OR GROUP GREED, HATRED, JEALOUSY, ENVY, DESPAIR, HOPELESSNESS, AND SO FORTH.

THE DEVIL HAS HIS GREATEST SUCCESS SEDUCING US AWAY FROM GOD BY WORKING WITH THE WAYWARD STIRRINGS OF OUR SPIRIT. Ideas like

- These people don't matter or count. My birth and status entitle me to more than them.

- I won't oppose this person or group even though **I know they are doing wrong (EVIL).**

- I want that and I'll take what I want. **It doesn't matter who it hurts.**

- I'll get away with an Evil act this time, or who cares, I'll do it anyway.

- Everyone else is doing this, why should I be different, even though I know its wrong.

- I'm superior to all of those people, they have no rights against me, who cares about them.

THE DEVILS GREATEST JOY COMES FROM RECRUITING US TO DO HIS EVIL WORK, BECOMING HIS SERVANT and DAMNING OURSELVES IN THE PROCESS

The Bible tells the story of how the Devil used Eve to tempt Adam, convincing Adam to follow her in sinning against God and demonstrated the cunning of the devil's lies to Eve.

Before the 2nd. World War, I believe the devil convinced Adolph Hitler that the Germans were the master race (Aryan Supremacy) who should rule the world making slaves of all other races. He convinced Hitler that the Jews were rodents and parasites who should be exterminated ignoring the fact that **our Lord Jesus Christ was a Jew.** The Devil helped Hitler gain absolute power in Germany and Hitler was his willing servant causing

1. The murder of SIX MILLION JEWS in German concentration camps.

2. The invasion of country after country.

3. World War 2 when after a long period of appeasement, the remaining free countries in the world were in fact forced to join and fight against these attempts at world domination.

4. The loss of MILLIONS OF LIVES ADDITIONAL TO THE JEWS ABOVE in people fighting the war and as a result of the war.

NAZI POWER WAS IMMENSE, DOMINATING and OVER POWERING AT ITS HEIGHT

Many individuals fought, were caught, tortured and laid down their lives in what must have seemed to be futile acts of heroism and self sacrifice opposing Nazi oppression before and during the 2nd. World war. **Opposition would have seemed hopeless, doomed to failure and required great courage and heroism from those who tried to oppose this evil.**

All good people who opposed Evil intense and overpowering with huge courage and heroism through our history set us examples of how to oppose evil. **They give us the hope that evil can be overcome and their stories show us how they did it.**

Evil gains strength from every sin committed, there are no

innocent sins, we choose to commit sins. We are however unaware of how quickly the sins we commit, combine with the sins being committed by all of us, which then escalate and accumulate bursting out to release evil---- intense, perverted, pervasive, depraved, addictive, cruel and overwhelming.

We must fight and oppose Evil whenever we encounter it. The survival of our souls for eternity is at risk if we don't. We don't have to be wowser s or do-gooders we need to obey God's commands to love Him and our fellow man. God wants us to succeed and will help us with every incident in our life. Our free will however allows us to choose exactly what we do or don't do. **Evil must be opposed and fought or it will triumph.**

Evil is much easier fought and repelled in its early stages and we are capable of rejecting it with our free will -----IF WE CHOOSE TO!

We sin when we do not reject evil. Non-action in fact condones the evil and helps it gain force and momentum with every sin committed. **Sin is always fun, alluring and attractive to us in its early stages. Its monstrous depravity, perversion, cruelty and addiction always soon appear and will overwhelm us if we do not fight against it.**

We must fight evil at every turn-------our eternal survival depends on this. Don't believe the Devil's lies or give in to his attempts to seduce and pervert us. Focus on God and His love and goodness to us and try to live your life helping God and our fellow men.

The Devil is evil incarnate and will do all in his power to take your soul away from God condemning it for eternity. -

WE HOWEVER MAKE OUR CHOICE TO SIN OR NOT TO SIN.

- CAUTION—There are many influential people, books and messages trying to convince us that there is no such entity as the Devil.-- THIS IS OF HUGE BENEFIT TO THE DEVIL

If we believe that there is no devil, then we are completely blind and open to His vicious manipulations, lies and efforts to promote our downfall.

DON'T BE DECEIVED, THE DEVIL IS THERE---EVIL INCARNATE------SEEKING US.

EVIL CAN BE OVERCOME, JUST REMEMBER
HOWEVER THAT IT DEPENDS ON US – BECAUSE.

- We are the soldiers!
- We are the fighters!
- We are the force required to defeat the evil that surrounds us!
- Don't cop out and expect others to do it for you! FIGHT, FIGHT, FIGHT with all your might to stop evil when ever and where ever it emerges

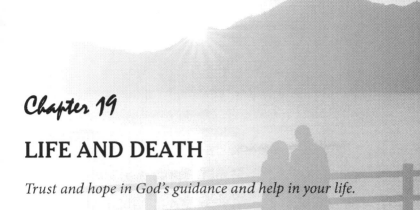

Chapter 19

LIFE AND DEATH

Trust and hope in God's guidance and help in your life.

How fragile, unstable and temporary our earthly lives are. Life is completely unpredictable, we are vulnerable in so many ways, we plan for our future, but what if it all collapses instantly. We may think our lives are stable, predictable and controllable, **But they are not, who knows what tomorrow will bring!**

Just think about people who get caught up, are directly, involved in and without any warning become a part of events like

- Earthquakes.
- Volcanic eruptions
- Fires, droughts, disease epidemics, plagues and pestilence
- Cyclones, hurricanes, tornado's etc.
- Tsunamis, tidal waves, floods
- **Accidents**---Aero plane, boat, train, bus, car, industrial, leisure, and so on.
- Murders, robberies, abductions, criminal acts
- Wars, rebellions, riots, terrorists acts, civil disturbances

- Asteroid or meteor strikes to our planet.

- **Any action either planned or random that sweeps us up and completely alters the content and course of our lives**

The only constant in our life is that-- it changes all the time—situations, people present, the resources we depend on and content of our lives-- **change all the time.**

We see world news reported and displayed on our television and computer screens. We invariably identify with the people involved who are killed, injured, lose hugely --physically, materially, mentally and are completely devastated by these events (not of their making and striking out of the blue) with complete surprise and devastation.

It does not take too much thought to realise that it could just as easily have been us who were involved and that we are vulnerable – 24/7 - to the unexpected.

We wipe our brows, say" PHEW "and are very glad that it was not us—**WE WERE SPARED this time, but what lies ahead? Only God knows- we can and must trust in our God and expect that even if we are involved, God will help, soothe and guide us through these trials.**

Viewing the big picture helps us keep our perspective and enables us to see that our earthly lives are insignificant compared with our eternal lives and the saving of our eternal lives is our fundamental priority. What happens here and now is only a part of the test we must pass through to gain our eternal life reward. Many people have advised me- **not to take myself too seriously**-This is good advice as it applies to all events in our earthly lives we can in most cases go with the flow. **We must however not take our eternal lives for granted and need to strive mightily to gain eternal happiness with our God. This is the fundamental purpose of our time on earth.**

NOTE: We cannot expect that our lives will be a continuous sequence of happy events. Jesus the innocent, sinless son of God endured huge pain, unfair abuse, torture, humiliation and death for our sake and in **obedience to His Father's will.** This did not however affect His eternal life, it only affected His earthly life. It appears that **our God wants us to realise that He created us and that we are dependent on Him, this is the truth and reality of our relationship with God.**

When all goes well and we enjoy ALL that God provides for us we quickly forget where all our abundance came from and the goodness and love that provided this. We start to believe that we are in control of All that happens in our lives.

"WRONG"— a reality check is required! ---Some disaster or severe test will occur either directly to us or to others, our fellow life travellers, which will test our obedience to God's will, our love and compassion for others and again show us the true reality of our existence.

All the pains and trials that we have to cope with in our earthly lives however, will fade into complete obscurity as eternity proceeds, - IF - we earn Heaven with our God.

The fact that our lives are unstable and unpredictable must not deter us from planning our life goals and striving for their accomplishment. Having a plan really helps us when we are involved in devastating and life changing events which force a complete re evaluation of our lives and what they now contain. Our original goals and plan however, do provide a starting point to help in our forced revaluation of what now matters in our life.

Our prime goal of saving our immortal souls however must not change, this is and will remain the fundamental purpose of our life here on earth.

Let us now consider death. Death is a fact of life, which we will (every one of us) have to face, endure and pass through -- **the ultimate end of our earthly life.**

Death acts like a great leveller or equaliser for the content of our life. It does not matter how powerful, rich or famous we were in our lives or how much other people – feared us - respected us - loved us - or hated us

When we die we will stand before God- completely bare- stripped of all our power, influence and material possessions. We take nothing with us except the knowledge and account of what we did in our earthly life, **the choices we made in our lives.**

My own personal near death experience and nearly everyone I know who has had a near death experience --- choking, drowning, suffocating, heart attack, etc. all experienced **GREAT FEAR at the point where one looses all control over what is happening and believe that death is imminent.** In spite of the fact that we did not die on this occasion, the intense fear, anxiety and complete loss of control over what was happening leaves one with no illusions, involuntarily we struggle and cling to life at the point of death and the process is terrifying.

I always thought that belief in God and belief in life after death with God would make the act of dying more or less painless and peaceful. This was untrue for me, I experienced great fear and this experience made me question the strength of my faith and in my belief that God would be present at and during my death providing peace and comfort.

Recognising and believing the fact that our earthly lives are very short, a mere blip in time when compared with eternity, you would think that we would not cling to our earthly life and that the step through death into eternal life should hold no fears for us. Logically this should be the case, however, practically (when death appeared imminent) I did not find this so, great fear and terror dominated and gripped me when I thought I was dying. These episodes have prompted me to pray to God for courage and peace the next time I am again confronted (probably at my actual death).

Logically and rationally our belief in God and a life hereafter should calm and comfort us at the vital moment of our death. Hopefully this will be so, still for me, this did not occur in my near death experiences and I pray that this changes

As previously stated in my books, I believe in a God who loves me. My life experience, the use of my thinking brain, the analysis of what I observed and was involved in - all confirmed and re assured me that God was there for me. **I derive great comfort from these thoughts.**

I realise again and again however, that **the Devil is active all the time and patiently waits to attack, he does this whenever we are vulnerable, trying desperately to take our faith away from us.** The fight is not over until it's over and the Devil will try hardest in these moments just before our death. He can alter completely our entry into eternity if we allow him to. We must be very alert and on our guard against these attacks, particularly when death is imminent, **don't let the Devil succeed at the moment when our victory is in sight.**

Logically and rationally, death should hold no terror for us if we have lived our lives as we believe God wants us to. Heaven and eternity with our God will be our reward, what then is there to fear? I believe the terrors I experienced were created by the Devil's lies and mighty efforts to create doubts and fears in my reality in this vital of moments.. I pray to God and trust that He will strengthen and protect me during this most critical time and enable me to gain the happiness and shared eternity with God that my soul craves.

Passage through death is our final earthly trial --- and -----Victory in this trial, will reward us with peace and happiness with our God, for all of eternity.

DEATH IS NOT THE END OF LIFE, BUT
THE START OF ETERNAL LIFE

TYING IT ALL TOGETHER

Trust and hope in God's guidance and help in your life.

Most people who believe in God worry and fret about the **exact details** of what **God is, has done and wants from us (letter perfect detail).** It's very sad that some possibly well intentioned believers exclude, persecute and condemn people who don't see God in precisely the same way as they do. **This has led to ALL the religious wars, persecutions and atrocities committed in God's name.**

Surely it is time to call a halt to these <u>**INSANE interpretations of God's will for us.**</u> God's relationship can be intensely personal and private with each of us, hence we should realise that---

WE HAVE NO RIGHT TO CONDEMN ANY OTHER PERSON FOR THEIR RELATIONSHIP WITH, AND UNDERSTANDING OF GOD.

HIS FUNDAMENTAL INSTRUCTIONS TO US ARE TO LOVE HIM AND OUR FELLOW MAN. THIS TRUTH MUST THEN PREVENT US FROM HARMING OTHERS FOR THEIR BELIEFS AND COMPREHENSION OF GOD.

WE sin against God when our actions kill and persecute our fellow man for how they believe and respond to God. What makes us right and them wrong, apart from our opinion. We have no right to condemn others for their heartfelt and deepest beliefs. We can share our beliefs as a comparison and a possible guide to them, but leave it at that.

I hope and trust that the contents of this book help each of you to serve God better, clarifying His fundamental instructions to all of us and alerting us to the blatant lies and manipulations of the Devil.

My efforts throughout this book have been to show you by logical thinking----

- That there is a God, the creator of us and of all that we perceive **"our consciousness, our reality "**.

- **That our God loves us with unconditional love.** That each and everyone of us is very important to Him. That **He knows each of us as individuals and each of us** can have a **personal relationship with Him**

- That God wants us to succeed in life and be happy, making the most of what we have been given.

- **That God demands that we love Him above everything and that we love our fellow men as we love ourselves.**

- That God has empowered and instructed chosen ones amongst us to teach us and lead us to Him. To provide us with details and laws as to how we should live our lives and provide us with living examples.

- **That God sent His son Jesus Christ into our world, the best and greatest of all of our teachers and leaders to show us how to accept God's will with patience and love as we live our lives.**

- **That our creation and existence (our life) is a test to see if we do love Him our God above all.** Do we choose Him with our free will and obey His commands to us?

- **That God's promise to us is happiness for all eternity if we follow His will.**

- That the Devil was Gods greatest creation GONE WRONG who rebelled against the God who created him, that he lost God's love for all eternity and now is so jealous of us because we have the opportunity to gain God's love for all eternity.

- **That the Devil will do all he can to cause us to fail and lose our opportunity of God's love forever. That the Devil is a master manipulator, LIAR, seducer and will try mightily to twist our beliefs in the reality we perceive to confuse us and turn us away from our God.**

- **That the Devil is EVIL INCARNATE— Doing his best to cause the damnation of our souls for eternity.**

- **That we have THINKING BRAINS (God's gift to us) which we can use to imagine, comprehend and plan our lives. That we have "free will" to choose what we do in our lives and that our choices determine**

WHAT HAPPENS TO US AFTER DEATH AND OUR PLACE IN ETERNITY.

I have tried to make this book non -denominational, even though I believe in the Christian version of God and try to live my life accordingly.

I do however believe that there is more than just one path to God. God in His mercy, I believe allows us freedom, within limits, to choose our path to God. We must however obey His will for us as we understand it, **complete Honesty and Sincerity are the Keys** as I believe our God looks into our souls and what they contain as a result of our lives.

I believe we are free to choose the religion that we follow and that it is very beneficial to us to choose an existing religion as these have invariably evolved from the thoughts, faith, and hope of sincere

followers of God. ---------We don't as it were have to "reinvent the wheel".

We are not unique (except to God) many have lived and died before us, millions of us live now and countless millions of us are yet to come. Yet each of us is an individual and very precious to God.

Our lives are our responsibility and we must answer for the choices we have made in our lives. It's never too late however to repent our sins and commit ourselves to our God.

I STRONGLY URGE YOU TO GIVE YOUR LIFE TO GOD, PICK THE RELIGION WHICH YOU BELIEVE IS RIGHT FOR YOU, ----- AND FOLLOW THIS FULLY AND COMPLETELY.

USE YOUR GOD GIVEN BRAIN TO ENSURE YOU ARE NOT LED ASTRAY BY OBSCURE PASSAGES THAT MAY BE WRITTEN, OR BY OTHERS INTERPRETATION AND PROCLAMATION OF WHAT IS WRITTEN.

GOD WANTS YOUR LOVE FOR HIM ABOVE ALL AND FOR YOU TO LOVE YOUR FELLOW MAN. -----ANYTHING CONTRARY TO THIS IS NOT GOD'S WILL.

I do not believe in RIGID DOGMA and ultra strict compliance with immovable letter perfect laws. As previously stated these result in complete abominations and obscenities of what God wants from us **we can learn from all who have lived and died before us, their whole life experiences and writings, especially those considered by some to be inspired by God. However do not follow these blindly switching off your thinking brain (God's gift to you) and acting on "the word" or someone's interpretation of the word.** This can result in suicide bombers, terrorists and practices completely contrary to what I believe our God wants from us.

Lots of issues in our lives are not black and white issues more shades of Gray, if you are not sure what God wants pray to Him and ask for His guidance, think intensely about what you are trying to decide-----**GOD WILL HELP YOU.**

A lot of us tend to be team players; we support our team with great feeling and intensity. There is nothing wrong with this except when it causes you to consider anyone outside the team as unworthy, inferior, unacceptable or so forth. God wants us to love all others as ourselves. I am a Catholic, you may be a Jew or a Moslem or whatever, I am sure some deceased members of all of our groups are with God in heaven and that He does not discriminate at all between them.

Love of God and sincere, earnest and honest efforts to do God's will are what is required.

We have no right to hate and want to injure or kill others. We do however have the right to defend ourselves against those who want to kill or injure us (or those who depend on us).

We must always however try to achieve love and support for others if it is at all possible. All of our lives are balancing acts and it is not always easy to maintain the balance, the middle road and moderation in everything, still **this is what we must strive for. Never forget that our life's purpose is to obey God's will for us and that our goals and objectives should serve this end.**

EVERYTHING AND ANYTHING IS POSSIBLE WITH GOD'S HELP.

TRUST IN GOD AND GOD'S HELP IS THE KEY TO SOLVING ALL OF OUR PROBLEMS.

When we think about our lives with out God as atheists, or people who have never been exposed to a belief in God, the concept of God in our lives is alien, strange and uncomfortable.

It is only when we open our thinking and attitude to the possibility

of God that we can feel and perceive His existence. We can experience great joy and comfort in the revelation that -

"We are not alone" and that we are loved, encouraged and supported by God in our lives and that our earthly lives are but a very short step to eternal life.

God poured out His healing, soothing grace to me in my life and this eased the pain mental and physical that my family and I endured.

Share in the JOY OF DISCOVERING GOD IN YOUR LIFE and realise that YOU can also find relief and peace for your sufferings both Physical – Pains and Handicaps and Mental – Anxieties, Fears, Despair and Depression.

Further more ALL OUR Earthly trials and pains will fade into oblivion when we achieve shared eternity with the God who created us.

I sincerely hope this book helps each of its readers to find God and make Him the most significant part of your life, and that you use the gifts and talents God has entrusted to you to bring yourself and as many of your life's companions back to the God, who has made us all, so that we can gain happiness with this God for all eternity.

May God bless us all!

Tony Lambert

Printed in the United States
By Bookmasters